in gratitude

This book started as a simple compilation of notes from countless home visits with families of infants. It then blossomed into an amazing journey with many people to whom I owe my gratitude for their contributions, insights, and support. I would like to thank the children—those who I have had the privilege of working with, observing, and learning from. I would like to thank the parents—those who have welcomed me into their homes, and the small group who reviewed the book throughout its production, especially Whitney Hegseth and Kate Raven who read and re-read countless versions with exceptional feedback. I would like to thank the educators—Dr. Montessori for her incredible wisdom, the Montessori practitioners who I have learned from and worked with, and to those who provided feedback and encouragement for this project, especially Lesley Monet Neustein, who read the earliest draft of the book and gave me critical input at that pivotal stage in writing, and the Grand Lake Montessori school for their sponsorship and enduring support of The PEACE Program. I would like to thank my team—the illustrators, Alisha Nicole Brumfield, Brenda Brambila, Esma Bošnjaković, Samantha Morales-Johnson, Sophia Marie Pappas, and Tracy Nishimura Bishop; the cover designer, Chie Ushio; the text editors, Amber Hatch and Elise Ramsbottom; and other contributors for their time, expertise, and talent. I would like to thank the backers of the Kickerstarter campaign that helped fund the illustrations in this book—the large-sum supporters will find their name embedded into the decorations on this page.

And, most importantly, I would like to thank my family—my immediate and extended family from as close as down the street to as far as Venezuela, my parents, especially my Mamá, Carmen Violich-Goodin, who was instrumental in guiding the graphic features of the book, and to my husband, Daniel, and my children, Solina and Harumoto—you three are my heart, and I love you always. You have all helped make this book the best version of itself, and I am deeply grateful to each of you. Thank you. —M.B.

Babies Build Toddlers
Copyright © 2020, 2021 by Mariana Bissonnette

Interior Illustrations copyright © 2020 by Alisha Brumfield, Brenda Brambila, Esma Bošnjaković, Samantha Morales-Johnson, Sophia Maria Pappas, and Tracy Nishimura Bishop. See "About the Illustrations" for more information about each illustrator's work in the book.

All rights reserved. No part of this book may be reproduced or used in any form or by any electronic or machanical means, without prior written permission of the copyright owner except for the use of brief quotations in a book review. For more information, contact the author at hello@babiesbuildtoddlers.com. Thank you for your support of the author's rights.

Library of Congress Control Number: 2020919300

ISBN: 978-0-578-75597-7 (hardcover)
ISBN: 978-0-578-85668-1 (paperback)

Cover design copyright © 2020 by Chie Ushio

Printed and bound in the United States of America

First published in hardcover in December 2020
First published in paperback in March 2021

www.babiesbuildtoddlers.com

BABIES BUILD TODDLERS

A Montessori Guide to
Parenting the First 18 Months

MARIANA BISSONNETTE

a letter to the reader

Hello! My name is Mariana Bissonnette, and I am a birth-to-six Montessori educator and parent of two. In my teaching, I've found it amazing to see the capacities and potentials of children in their earliest years—it truly is an unparalleled time of growth and importance. But when I became a parent, I struggled. I felt overwhelmed, vulnerable, and just *so* tired. I knew as an educator that these early years were incredibly important for my children, and yet I found them *so* difficult as a parent. How were parents supposed to manage? How could we help our children reach their potential during such a trying time?

More often than not these days, we are parenting in isolation, and as such, are looking for a community to lean on during this early time. But while finding (or creating) support is essential for parents, it doesn't address the other half of our problem: the child and their important development. Physician-turned-educator Dr. Maria Montessori considered this dilemma many years ago and came up with a solution: an *assistant* to infancy.[1] This assistant would be an educator equipped with the knowledge of child development, the materials to support it, and the time to assist parents during these formative first few years. In this way, parents would have the support *and* the information to help their child reach their potential. Sounds amazing, right? Right!

After earning my 0–3 Montessori certification, I became this "assistant" by starting a community program called PEACE *(Parent Education and Child Empowerment)*. In this program, I have facilitated a weekly drop-in support group for new parents, visited families in their homes (in person and virtually) for personalized consultations, and conducted parenting workshops about the intersection between development, education, and parenting. It was in this new role that I saw how truly powerful this model was. When parents were given more support, they had more time and energy to meet the developmental needs of their children. And when children's developmental needs were being met, they became remarkably easier to parent. It was this amazing positive feedback loop whereby supporting one, you supported the other. Win-win-win. In an effort to extend this support to more families than I could possibly meet in person, I wrote *Babies Build Toddlers*. My aim is to make developmental information accessible through a visual guide to the first 18 months.

Land Acknowledgement

The community work that informed the writing of this book and the place in which it was written is on the unceded territory of Huchuin, part of the ancestral land of the Lisjan Ohlone people who traditionally speak the language Chochenyo (Oakland, CA). If you live in the San Francisco Bay Area, I hope you join me in contributing to the Shuumi Land Tax, a voluntary financial contribution that non-indigenous residents can make to support the acquisition and preservation of local land for Indigenous people. If you live outside of the San Francisco Bay Area, I encourage you to find, honor, and acknowledge the Native Land you live on.

This Moment in Time

This book was finalized during the COVID-19 pandemic and the international solidarity with the Black Lives Matter movement against the persistence of police brutality, racism, and white supremacy. These moments have laid bare racism's deep roots and the policies that uphold them, but also the essential voices of Black and Indigenous Leaders who have long been doing the work of moving us as a society toward an anti-racist future. As a white[2] author, I wanted to acknowledge that in the role of "author," my voice—a white voice—is being centered and amplified. Too often, the amplification of white voices is at the cost of hearing the voices of Black, Indigenous, and People of the Global Majority.[3] I therefore implore you to start your parenting journey elsewhere and listen to the voices of the educators and advocates in and out of the Montessori community who are guiding us toward anti-bias/anti-racist education for all, from birth. This list is just a start and I hope your list grows as mine surely will, too:

- **Britt Hawthorne**: www.britthawthorne.com
- **Daisy Han**: www.embracingequity.com
- **Dr. Kira Banks**: www.raisingequity.com
- **Tiffany Jewell**: www.anti-biasmontessori.com; *This Book Is Anti-Racist* (2020)
- **Trisha Moquino**: www.indigenouscheerleader.com; www.kclcmontessori.org

A portion of the proceeds from this book will go toward expanding 0–3 Montessori training opportunities for aspiring Black, Indigenous, and Montessorians of the Global Majority. I hope you join me in contributing to the Black Montessori Education Fund, the Indigenous Montessori Institute or other like organizations and foundations. I am grateful to have you here, and hope you enjoy it!

—*Mariana Bissonnette, July 13, 2020*[4]

"... how, in a practical sense, can we educate a newborn baby, or even an infant during the first two years of his life? What lessons shall we give to this tiny being who understands nothing of what we say, and cannot even move his limbs? Or do we mean only hygiene, when we speak of this little one's education? Not at all. We mean far more than that ... "

—Maria Montessori, *The Absorbent Mind* [5]

acknowledgements & introduction illustrations by:

sophia marie pappas

introduction

Imagine that you had two items in front of you and I asked you to pick the one that was best for your baby: a developmental toy proven to increase cognitive function . . . or the box the toy came in. Aside from extolling the virtues of playing with an empty box, you'd probably think the first one is the better toy, right? Wrong! But you'd be wrong with the box, too. You see, the answer isn't actually an answer; it's a question (a couple of questions, actually):

How old is the child? What is the child doing developmentally? What is the child interested in? Is there anything preventing the child from using either toy?

Though you are likely reading this book because you want answers to your questions, it is not the answers themselves that are inherently supportive to the child. Rather, it is the understanding of the development *behind* those answers that yields the most support. Understanding this development is about following the *story* of the child—where they've been, where they are, and where they're going. As such, this book is meant to read like a novel—from the first page onward. And just as you can't skip ahead in development, try not to skip ahead in this book. Stay with the story of the child, and that story will stay with you. This is what will help you answer your own questions and is the framework of Montessori education.

Montessori is a developmental approach to education as an aid to life.[6] The guiding principles center on understanding the child's development, preparing ourselves and our child's spaces to best support that development, and then observing the child in front of us to see that development unfold. The ideas presented in this book are based on my Montessori trainings, my experience as an educator and as a parent, and my own work with families and infants just like yours. And as you learn about development and watch your child grow, you will probably draw some of your own conclusions as well (and I hope you do!). Thankfully, Dr. Montessori and her colleagues were kind enough to do much of this legwork for us (thanks, Maria!). Furthermore, you will find extensive references and citations in the back for further reading (see pp. 128–139). So, let's get started with our one basic principle of development:

babies build toddlers . . .

babies build toddlers

Children develop by building themselves over a series of successive stages that stack on top of one another like a tower (something Dr. Montessori referred to as "self-construction"[7]). But unlike a tower that starts from a base and is built upward, the foundational period of the first three years is much more like the growth of a seed.[8]

A seed grows in a hole in the ground and incubates for some time. This is like pregnancy. The seed is nourished by the conditions that surround it, just like the fetus is nourished by the mother's body. Despite developing rapidly, neither the seed nor the fetus are visible.

In a burst of life, the seed's roots descend into the nutrient-rich soil. This mirrors birth and the first 18 months of infancy. The roots are building a foundation that will have life-long effects on the health and well-being of the plant. The work is active, but again largely unseen by us. So, too, with the infant—despite actively constructing their foundation, much of their work goes unnoticed. If we try to prod, push, test, and demand visible growth, we risk pulling the roots from the very foundation they are trying to create. Instead, we must trust that we have created sufficient conditions for the roots to grow.

In a second burst of life, the seed sprouts through the earth. This is like toddlerhood. The sapling bursts from the ground, young and newly independent. It is not yet robust, as even the leaves droop down at first, but it is visible and active. When the young toddler arrives, we see personality, language, and capacity, but also vulnerability and tenderness. Like the newly emerged plant, we are excited to finally see a glimpse of the young person they are becoming.

You see, we grow down before we grow up. The child's development in the first three years is so expansive we might wonder how a child so young manages to accomplish all of this! Well, let's take a look at the top four "powers" (as Dr. Montessori called them) of infancy.

Genetics

Our DNA provides the instructions we are born with that tell our bodies what to develop at what time. This is why we have a (mostly) predictable path of human development: most children sit at around six months and walk at around a year. But we also know that every child develops along their own path within these basic timelines. It is, therefore, up to the child's unique genetic instructions and their experiences to create their individual path of development.

Experiences

The brain develops like the roadways of a city. The most traveled roads get the most attention (paving, clear signage, etc.) and are therefore the most popular to use because they are the most efficient. The brain's neural network works similarly: the more the child experiences something, the stronger and more efficient that "roadway" becomes. The brain then uses the most efficient pathways to function, so it is essential to have a strong network to build a well-functioning brain.

The Absorbent Mind

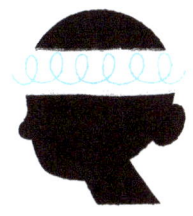

It is one thing to experience something, and quite another to absorb all of the information the brain received during that experience. That's where the special ability Dr. Montessori called "The Absorbent Mind"[9] comes into play. This is the unique ability of the young child to absorb everything they experience and make it part of themselves (she described this as "incarnation"[10]). During this period, we would be wise to use the kinds of actions and words we want our child to absorb.

Sensitive Periods

If the all-absorbent mind isn't focused on anything in particular, it can be hard to acquire the specific skills we need to be successful adults. "Sensitive periods" (also called "critical periods"[11]) act like a spotlight to create that focus. For example, we absorb all of the sounds around us, but because we focus our attention on the human voice (within the sensitive period for language), we learn to talk. Recognizing these periods will help us see what the child is focused on, so that we can best support them in acquiring those skills.

sensitive periods examined

Dr. Montessori originally got the idea for "Sensitive Periods" by studying the work of a biologist, Hugo DeVries,[12] who noticed that caterpillars had a special sensitivity to light when they were young. By being sensitive (or attracted) to light, the young caterpillars were motivated to leave the safety of the center of the plant and eat the soft leaves at the plant's edges. Once they had grown older and their jaws had matured, this sensitivity faded and they stayed in the safe center of the plant. These periods of attraction (or sensitivity) helped focus the caterpillar on acquiring a specific skill (jaw maturity). Dr. Montessori observed similar sensitivities in children in the first six years of life, most notably: movement,[13] language,[14] and order.[15] Sensitive periods overlap and are transitory (meaning their intensity fades in and out).[16] Therefore, despite being predictable, they are not always easy to disentangle one from another. To have the privilege of noticing them, we must therefore understand how they manifest.

movement

If *you* get up during mealtimes in infancy, *your child* will get up during mealtimes in toddlerhood. By being aware of the sensitivity toward movement, we can model what we want our child to absorb. The focus of this sensitive period is on learning foundational, voluntary movements. It lasts until about six years of age.

language

If you *show* a child how to do something (movement) at the same time as you *explain* how to do it (language), the child is likely losing half of the information because they are trying to focus on both. Best practice, therefore, is to show, and *then* explain. This sensitivity's focus is on acquiring language. It lasts for about six years.

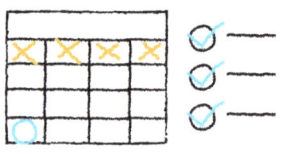

order

This sensitive period's function is to classify and categorize all of the inputs the brain receives. This includes a focus on physical order as well as in the predictability of routine ("temporal order"). It lasts from about 1–3 years of age.[17] Knowing this can help you set up your spaces and time to be mostly predictable.

the most important page in the book

Between the child's efforts, and what is already present, it can be hard for us to fully understand our role. Because rather than being "teachers" who must instruct the child on how to develop, we are guides[18] who know that these instructions come built in. We are therefore like the gardeners whose essential task is to create the sufficient conditions that allow the plant to grow. So, let's consider how best we can perform this role depending on whether we are supporting the essential developments (the roots) or the environment that ensures their robust growth (the conditions):

Your Role & the Roots

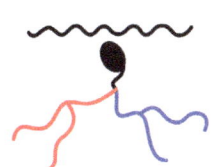

The roots are what the brain and body are focused on developing (like the seed is focused on growing a plant). In infancy, the child's developmental focuses are on coordinating their *movement* and building *language*. You cannot learn movement or language for your child; your child needs to learn these for themselves. The child, for example, does not need to be "taught" to crawl; they just move their body until they do. Your essential role, therefore, is to *not block* the child from developing language or movement and to *inspire* them to move and talk even more.

Your Role & the Conditions

The conditions ensure that the roots can grow (like the soil, water, and sun function for the plant). For people, this is *food* (the fuel), *sleep* (the processing of development), and *hygiene* (how we avoid illness). The child cannot initially do these tasks for themselves, but they can once their bodies mature. For example, the caretaker feeds the child, and then later the child can feed themselves. At some point we need to *transfer* responsibility for meeting this need. Your role is to meet these needs for the child while they can't, and then *let them take over* once they can. It is essential to follow the developmental timeline of these "transfers" so that the child can participate as soon as they are able.

Babies Build Toddlers has been organized around these roots and conditions, with each section following them over the first 18 months. Let's take a look!

"The brain grows more during the [first] 1,000 days than at any other period of life. The basic architecture of the brain, which provides a foundation for all future learning, behavior, and health, is constructed through an ongoing process that begins before birth and continues into adulthood."

—Roger Thurow, *The First 1,000 Days* [19]

table of contents

1. **The Plant:**   15
   The Toddler That Babies Build

2. **The Roots:**   21
   The Child's Developmental Focus

3. **The Conditions:**   57
   What the Child Needs to Grow

4. **The Gardener:**   103
   The Adult's Essential Role

5. **The Full Chart:**   117
   Putting it Together: Birth to 18 Months

"The one thing life can never do is to stand still. Independence is not a static condition; it is a continuous conquest . . . The child's first instinct is to carry out his actions by himself, without anyone helping him, and his first conscious bid for independence is made when he defends himself against those who try to do the action for him."

—Maria Montessori, *The Absorbent Mind*[20]

the plant:
the toddler that babies build

chapter illustrations by:

brenda brambila *(me!)*   esma bošnjaković *(I do it!)*   tracy nishimura bishop *(maximum effort)*

the toddler that babies build

We are going to start our story at the end instead of the beginning, because it can be hard to create the essential conditions for this seed if we don't know what kind of plant we are growing. What is it supposed to look like? How much sun does it need? And how much room does it need to grow?

So, what does this toddler look like? What capacities are they trying to build? And what foundation will allow them to realize their potential? As it turns out, there are three very important developmental milestones that show up right at the transition to toddlerhood. Looking at these can help us address these important ideas:

me!

I do it!

maximum effort

me!

In toddlerhood, the word "me" enters into the child's vocabulary.[21] This is the child telling the world, "I see myself as my own person!" You see, this hasn't always been clear. The child started life in utero where the line between "you" and "me" was blurred (at best!) and even after birth, they were still very much attached and dependent on you. And while this interplay between the self and the community is a constant throughout life with each shaping the other, the declaration of "me" is a moment of clarity for the child about their own agency in life. By respecting that they have always had their own thoughts, choices, and preferences from birth, we are best positioned to support their growing sense of self in toddlerhood. In this book, I call this "identity," which is meant to embody both one's own self and the community that continually shapes it.

i do it!

Also in toddlerhood, the child asserts themselves and demands that they start doing everything for themselves.[22] The burden of responsibility for meeting their needs has not always been clear. In the womb, the child's needs were met without them lifting a finger; they were given nutrients directly from the umbilical cord and lived in near-perfect conditions. After birth, their needs were still met by you, but the child then needed to actively communicate those needs. Over time, as the child built capacity, they started meeting some of their needs themselves. When the child asserts "I do it" (in their actions or their words), they are really saying, "I should be the one to meet my needs now (not you!)." If we allow the child to do what they are capable of doing from birth, we can create the roots of capacity to back up their insistence that they do things themselves (because then they actually can). In this book, I call this "capacity."

maximum effort!

Toddlers will reliably seek out the most impossible tasks—from trying to lift the heaviest bag of groceries to trying to push a cart full of rocks. This is the developmental moment when the child believes they can do hard things. This is the attitude and drive they need to accomplish all of the independent skills they seek to acquire. When the child exerts maximum effort,[23] they are really saying, "I will put in the effort and hard work needed to do it all." If we can support their motivations and interests from birth, they will create the roots they need to overcome difficulties and become as capable as they are trying to be. In this book, I call this "perseverance."

summary

You see, toddlerhood is the burst of the seed from the ground; it is life's thrust out of infancy and into childhood. It is a window of opportunity where the child has the drive and motivation to take charge of themselves. This opportunity is maximized when this toddler can stand on a strong foundation of skills and knowledge from infancy that directly supports these upcoming developments. It may seem a long way off now, but supporting the toddler starts by supporting the infant.

We will therefore follow these three core ideas—identity, capacity, and perseverance—as we look at the particular developmental roots of the first 18 months and the conditions that support their growth.

What supports <u>identity</u> during infancy:
See the infant as a person with their own interests, needs, thoughts, and choices from birth. This way, the child grows up with their own sense of agency about their budding life so they don't have to demand it in toddlerhood.

What supports <u>capacity</u> during infancy:
Let the child do what they are capable of doing . . . as soon as they can do it! This way, when they insist that they can do things themselves around 18 months, they actually can.

What supports <u>perseverance</u> during infancy:
Follow their motivations and interests from birth. This way, when the child exerts maximum effort, they have the perseverance to push through obstacles and succeed.

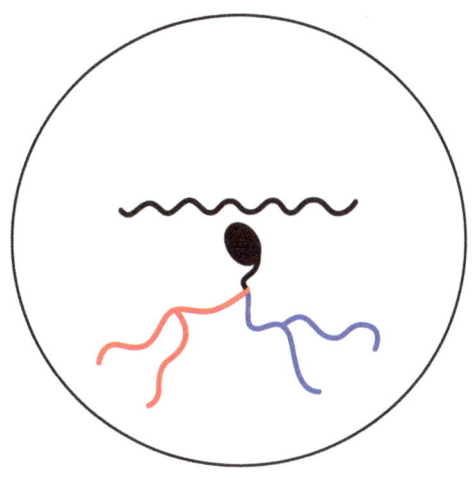

the roots:

the child's developmental focus

illustrations by:

samantha morales-johnson esma bošnjaković

introduction to the roots

Welcome to the roots! Here you will ground yourself in the developments of both movement and language. Each section will follow this outline:
- Why this development matters
- The timeline of this development
- What inspires *more* of this development
- What limits this development
- This development and the budding toddler

Quick Reminders About "the Developments":
- **The Developments**: This is what the brain and body are focused on in infancy
- **Role of the Adult**: These are things we cannot do for the child. They do these for themselves from the start.
- **Activities and Materials**: The aim of the activities and materials (toys) that we give to the child should be to inspire or stimulate more of the development (and not obstruct it). So, for example, let's say you get a fantastic rattle for your baby and they want to play with the box the rattle came in; the box, in this instance, would be more important because it is inspiring the child to coordinate their movements to grasp it. When we respect their interests (identity), they improve their skills (capacity) and will use their interests to drive their motivation to overcome obstacles (perseverance).

Timelines:
As we go through each development, I will outline the average expected milestones in a series of timelines with the child's age in months along the top, like the chart of the sensitive periods below. Do note that these are *general* timelines based on due date (not birth date). If you have questions or concerns about your child's development, however, you should consult your child's medical provider.

	birth	*6 mo*	*12 mo*	*18 mo*
Sensitive Periods*	Movement (Birth–6 Years)			
	Language (Birth–6 Years)			
*This represents only some of the sensitive periods				Order (1–3 Years)

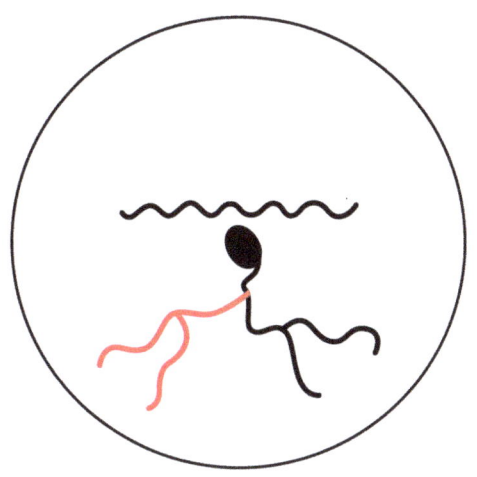

movement:

the first root

illustrations by:

samantha morales-johnson

why movement matters

Movement will be our first root because without movement, nothing else is possible —no talking, no self-soothing, no playing, no . . . nothing![24] In fact, while many might think that the brain is wired to *learn*, the brain is actually wired to *move*.[25] Learning is just an outcome of how we interact (move) with our environment. So, let's consider how to support and maximize movement with your child.

Time

There is a fatty sheath called "myelin" that protects the signals sent between the brain and the body.[26] It's like the casing around an electrical wire, protecting the electricity from the outlet to a lamp. Without this protection, the electricity would never get to its destination. The same is true for the body; until something is myelinated, the brain can't control it because the signal keeps getting lost. You can tell if the myelin has reached an area of the body when the child can control those muscles (i.e. myelin has reached the neck once the child can hold up their head). Myelin in the body grows from top to bottom, and in to out, (or head to feet, and torso to hands).[27] This is why we roll (shoulders), and then sit (back), and then crawl (knees), and then walk (feet). Not everyone grows myelin at the same rate.

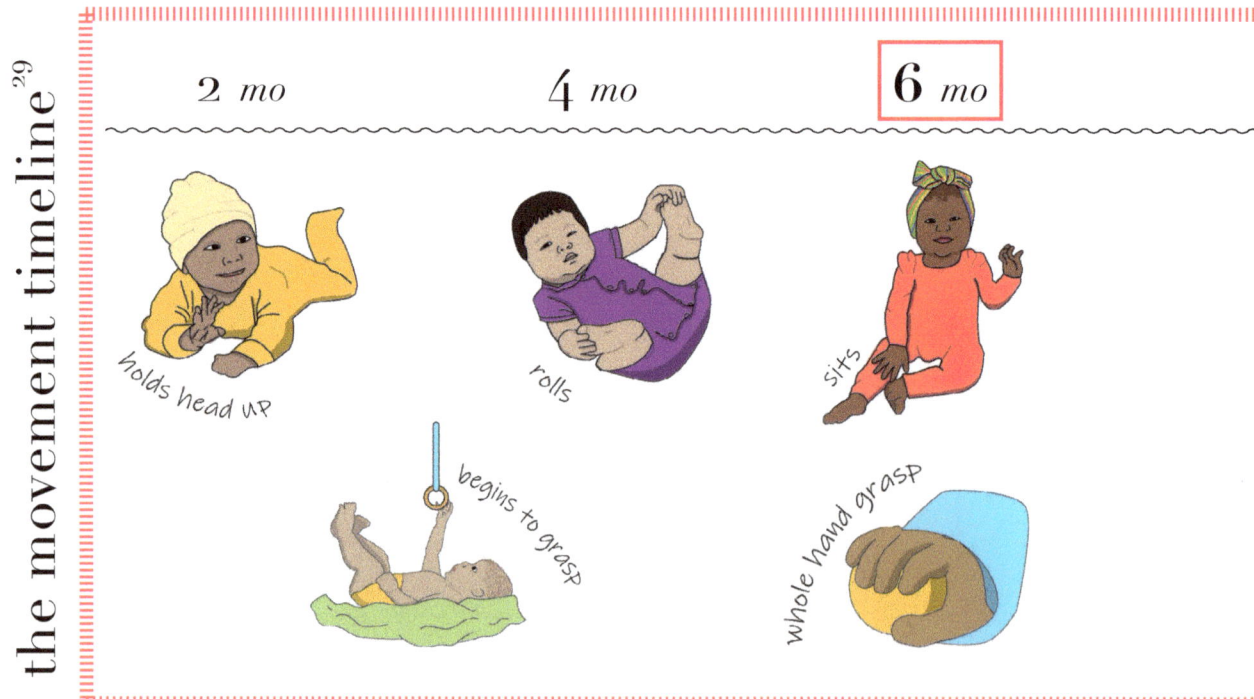

the movement timeline[29]

2 mo — holds head up
4 mo — rolls, begins to grasp
6 mo — sits, whole hand grasp

Practice

Practice makes perfect, right? Right! And the best way to practice motor movements is to, well . . . move! It might sound obvious, but if we think about how much of the day the child has the ability to move their body freely, it might be less than we want. Giving the child safe, unrestricted floor time is the best way to allow them to develop their motor coordination. This means yes to the floor, and no to fitted chairs or jumpers, and limited time in swaddles, strollers, baby carriers, or car seats. The point is that when you let them move (capacity), they will be able to.

Interest

Toys are only worth their salt if they are inspiring more movement (not less).[28] But how do you inspire movement in a child who has barely any motor control, let alone the ability to see what you give them? Well, rather than *waiting* until their motor skills are more mature to give them something to do, just adjust their spaces and toys to the motor skills they *do* have. This might mean dangling a mobile above a newborn instead of handing them a rattle they cannot grasp. Or it might mean giving a non-crawling child a stationary toy. By making their toys *accessible*, they develop their interests from the start. This is what gives them the motivation to gain new skills, even when it's hard (perseverance).

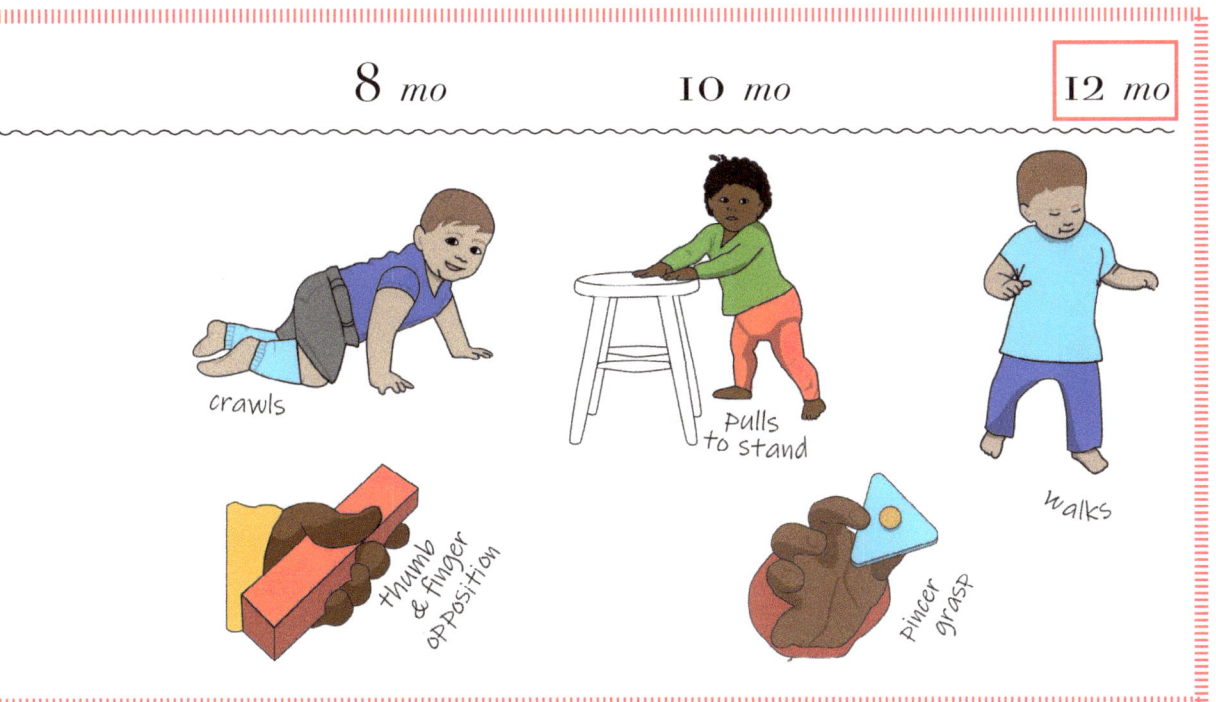

setting the space to inspire movement

Using the child's expected motor developments to inform how we set up our spaces might sound great, but sometimes it can be hard not to get lost in the paralyzing amount of developmental information out there! So, let's use some "big picture" ideas to inspire movement in your space.

The Three Trimesters of Movement

You may have noticed in the Movement Timeline (see pp. 24-25) that infancy had marked transition points for the next phase at sitting and walking (or 6 and 12 months of age). These particular motor milestones are important because they change the body's position to be more upright and thus, change the kinds of spaces and toys that will interest the child. Before sitting, the child's interests are mostly in things that are dangled from above (because that's where they are looking). Once they can sit, however, their interests change to what is in front of them: where the toy is, where it goes when it's dropped, how it interacts with other toys, etc. And finally, once upright and mobile, the child's interests revolve around moving (first themselves, and then their toys) from one place to the next.

All the Child *Can* Do is All the Child *Should* Do

What might be less noticeable in this timeline is how movement unfolds over time. In order to *do* any new motor move, the child simply needs to continue practicing their *current* motor skills. They do not need to be propped to sit in order to sit, nor do they need to be "taught" to roll or crawl in order to roll or crawl.

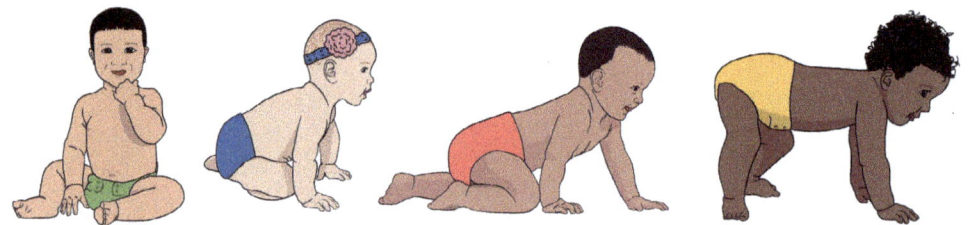

Developing neck strength is what allows the child to steady their head as they roll. Rolling is what shores up the core strength to sit. Sitting, rather than lying on their tummy, is the beginning of crawling, because the child leans forward until they can. Remember, the child needs no instructions. Our job is to *allow* the unobstructed movements the child can currently do and to inspire them to move even more!

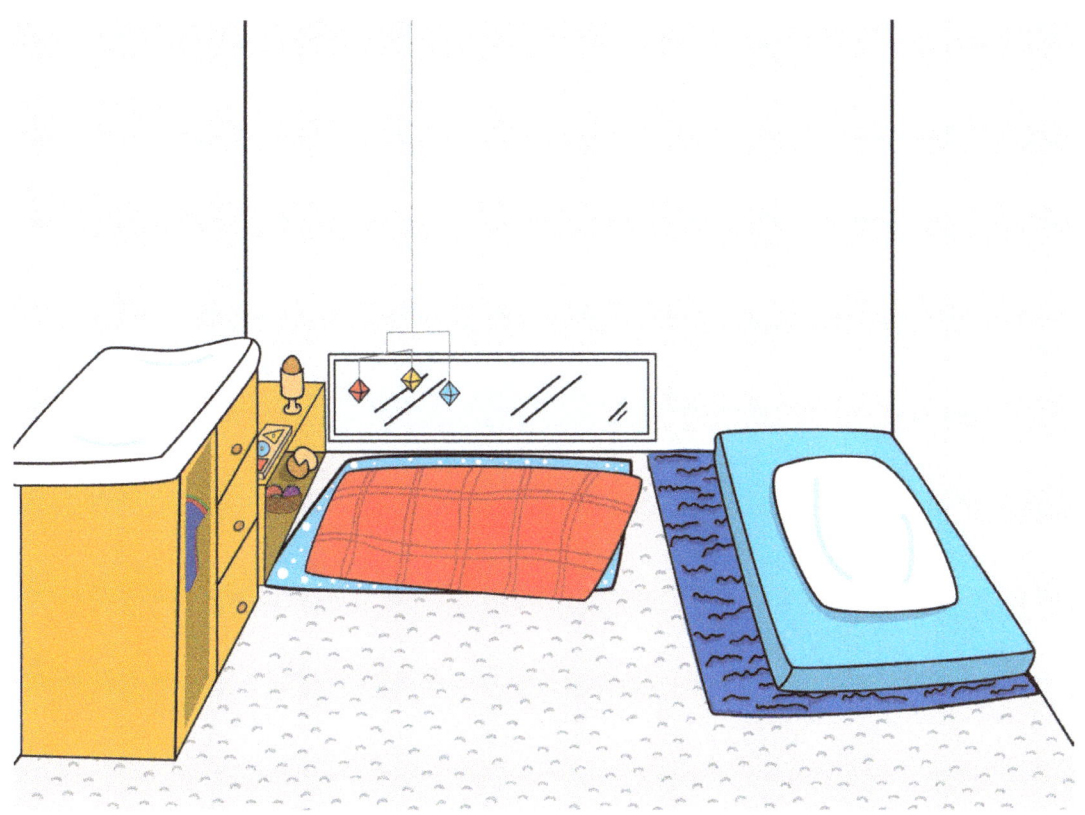

less is more

Let's remember the "absorbent mind" (see p. 9). This is the idea that the child is absorbing everything all at once. That means that if you have music on, are making dinner, and leave stimulating toys all around—that crinkle, light up, are multi-colored, and that have various textures—the child can get over-stimulated very quickly. Less is much more.

purpose & place

The basic layout of the child's space can include specific, purposeful materials to meet their needs[30]: a place for eating, sleeping, hygiene/self-care, and movement. If we limit their space to only include items that have a clearly defined purpose, it can aid the child in seeing where to meet their needs and help us avoid cluttering the child's space.

accessibility

What the child cannot access, the child cannot use. When we make the child's toys and materials accessible on low, open shelves (instead of toy bins), the child's choices are clear, which inspires their use. This also supports the adult in limiting the number of toys for the child as toy bins tend to accumulate far more things than the infant will use.

inspiring movement: birth to sitting

Life before sitting has a lot to do with the view, and the ability to see that view. For the sighted child, they look up most of the time and focus on close objects:

	birth	2 mo	4 mo	6 mo
Eyesight[31]	Range of 7-30"	Tracks objects	Depth perception & color maturation	

When considering what might inspire movement before sitting, you can see how limiting the child's experience is with handheld toys: they tend to drop whatever we give them, can't roll over to go get them, and don't even know what they're missing. Dangled toys, on the other hand, are still there even when they're dropped. Plus, when you hang toys at the right distance (see the above timeline), the child will focus on them and be inspired to work toward reaching them (perseverance).

The Truth About Tummy Time

When we meet the child where they are, instead of getting frustrated with where they aren't, their skills grow (capacity). "Tummy time" is the practice of laying a baby on their stomach when awake so that they can strengthen muscles they don't use while lying on their back (a position they are in most often). But most parents bemoan that their child hates this! So, let's get one thing straight: *every baby hates tummy time* . . . at a certain point. You see, while most blame the "tummy," what's more to blame is the "time." Tummy time is hard work! Instead of seeing it as something your child hates, think of it as something they can do for however long they can. Remember that this is about giving the child the *opportunity* to use their neck muscles, and they can do this in a baby carrier, on your chest or legs, etc.

Independent Play vs. Engaged Play

"Independent play" (when the child entertains themselves) and "engaged play" (when the adult entertains the child) are both important opportunities to support the child's roots. For the most part, independent play is an opportunity to grow the root of movement because the child is directing their interests and movements without interruption. The child is often the most interested in independent play right after waking and eating. Once these basic needs have been met (and they are properly burped!), try laying the child down in a comfortable place for movement, take a step back and let them explore for however long they want.

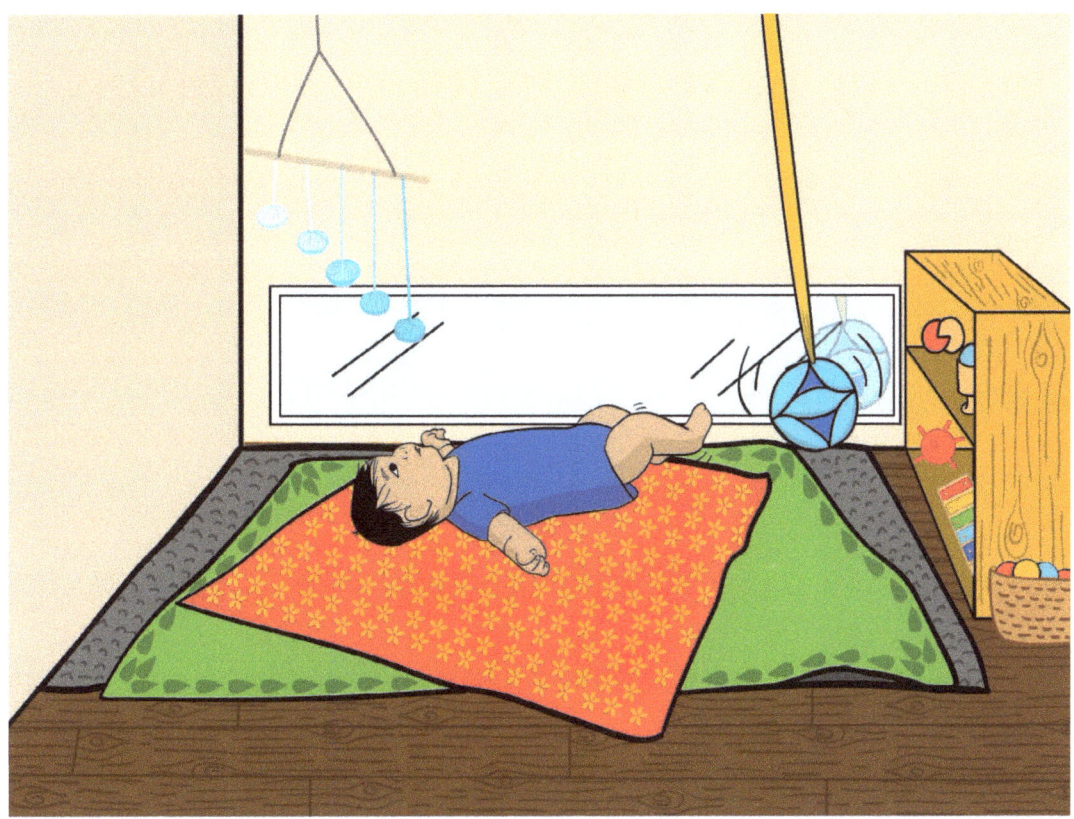

the mat & the mirror

The first item on the play space checklist is a comfortable mat.[32] Mats can be smooth or textured, just so long as the child can move freely and safely. In addition, a low, *real* mirror[33] hung horizontally along the child's play space is a fantastic addition. At a time when the child is developing neck strength, it can often be hard to turn toward sounds or sights that might be interesting to them. The mirror allows the child to see the whole room even without the ability to turn their head. It is also an aid to tummy time as they love seeing themselves as they lift their head!

the mobiles

The child will be inspired to move when they have something hung at a distance they can see, and later reach, and that they can't lose if it's dropped. Mobiles[34] can really be anything that is dangled from above. These can be traditional mobiles, like those common in Montessori spaces: the Munari, the Gobbi (pictured), or the Takane Kicking Ball (pictured). Alternately, mobiles can be a carefully placed plant whose leaves extend over the play space. Once the child is grasping, mobiles that are meant to be touched, like a teething ring on a ribbon, are fast favorites.

inspiring movement: sitting to walking

Sitting changes the child's whole worldview as they are now upright and can start to see sequence much more clearly (*"So that's where my toy goes when I drop it!"*). This contributes to the realization that a hidden object is still there ("object permanence"). And when the child starts to crawl, they become painfully aware that you are around somewhere even when they can't see you. This provokes some real anxiety about being away from you ("separation anxiety").[35]

	6 *mo*	8 *mo*	10 *mo*	12 *mo*
Cognitive Milestones		Object permanence & separation anxiety		*(Separation anxiety continues)*

Now, "separation anxiety" can easily be interpreted as the child being anxious because they like you so much and have just realized that they can be away from all your awesomeness. This interpretation, however, not only puts the adult at the center of the problem (being away) and therefore the solution (coming back), but it also largely misses (and impedes) a crtitical root of perseverance: self-confidence. You see, the child isn't just anxious to be away from *you*, they are anxious to be away from what you *represent*. You are a person who has been meeting their needs their whole life. When they are away from you, they are wondering if they are going to be alright. By preparing their spaces so that they *are* alright, they start to believe that they are, too (what Montessori called the "second basic trust").[36]

Safe and Free Exploration

Safe and free exploration of the child's world is an essential component in the development of self-confidence.[37] In a space prepared for the child's free explorations (as opposed to a pen or play yard), the child can use their mobility to start to meet their needs *("I missed Mommy so I went and found her,"* or *"My gums hurt so I got a teether,"* or even *"I was tired so I went to bed")*. If we routinely stop the child from exploring because the space isn't prepared *("Oh, not that, that's Daddy's book! Whoops, not the lamp!")* or quarantine the child off to the side in a pen or play yard, we inadvertently tell the child that they need to be "saved" *("I guess I'm not alright!")* or that they can't trust their space *("I should stay with you!")*. This can prolong separation anxiety and lower the child's self-confidence. If instead we remove or relocate potential hazards, we will be confident in their exploration (and they will be, too). This is essential to perseverance.

a low, open shelf

Keep in mind that *less is more*, especially for the mobile child who needs a considerable amount of open (uncluttered) floor space to explore. In using a low, open shelf to display a few (4–6) toys, the child will start to orient to where their toys can be found. This helps the child meet their needs more quickly and lays a foundation for putting their toys away later. Moreover, mobiles lose their appeal as the sitting child is looking down more than up. Try adding handheld toys that offer a sequence (like a puzzle, stacking rings, or a xylophone) for added interest.

discovery drawers

By allowing children to discover new and interesting things in the home, they develop the learning disposition that the world is full of interesting things to do (they just have to find them). Moreover, mobile babies are curious and get into *everything* within their reach. Lean into this by having "discovery drawers" in various places in the home. For example, you might add a child lock to most of the drawers/cabinets in the kitchen, but leave one unlocked with a few safe kitchen items in it (spatula, measuring cups, etc.). Don't show the child the drawer; let them discover it!

inspiring movement: walking to 18 mo

Walking marks the onset of toddlerhood. The child's body is now fully upright, which means their hands are free in their movements. This new ability to walk and hold onto something at the same time translates into one of the early toddler's favorite activities: moving something from one place to another. But how do we foster *this* interest to inspire *more* movement? Remember the sensitive periods?

The Emergence of the Sensitive Period of Order

Somewhere between 12–18 months, the child will *all of a sudden* be deeply disturbed by something that is "out of place." This might be a jacket that isn't where it is "supposed to be"[38] or a missing plant that had always been in a particular place;[39] or a once-whole banana that has broken in half. It may appear as though your angel infant has turned into a terrible toddler overnight: melting down because things didn't go "their way." This interpretation, however common, is largely missing the point. The child isn't upset because things weren't how they *wanted*, they are upset because things weren't how they *expected*—and that's a big difference. Consider your home and the sensible, predictable places you've put your belongings. You keep keys by the door, cooking tools in the kitchen, and toilet paper in the bathroom. Why? Because having a predictable order allows you to meet your needs—and it does for the child, too. The child's distress, therefore, is about not knowing how to meet their needs when their environment is unpredictable. We can temper these tantrums by creating an orderly space for the child to use where they can start to create that order themselves.

Putting Their Things Away

A perfect marriage between the child's heightened focus on order and their interest in moving things from one place to another is putting their things away. This is not only the favorite trait of any roommate ever, but it allows the child to create the order necessary to meet their needs. Let's take a look at how to guide this:

- **Tell them** what is about to happen: *"Let's put the blocks away!"*
- **Show them** an example: *"Look! This block goes in this box."*
- **Give them an Opportunity** to do it: *"You can put a block in the box!"*
- **Wait, then Acknowledge**: Give them time to respond. If they do it, say: *"You put the block in the box!"* If they don't, *happily* return to step one (Tell them).

a table & chair

With their new upright posture, the child spends less time playing and working on the floor, and you might notice them playing directly at a shelf. To support the child in using a surface suitable for their activity, try adding a low table and chair[40] to their play space. By giving their activity a place to be brought to, the child adds a layer of sequence to their work *("I choose something, take it somewhere, use it, and put it back")*. It is important to get a table and chair that properly fit the child's body with their feet flat on the floor and their knees bent at a 90-degree angle.

practical life

The manipulative toys that the child used from 6–12 months that offer an extended sequence continue to be quite popular from 12–18 months. But often, the most exciting activities for the newly walking child are the things they see *you* do every day (what Dr. Montessori called "practical life").[41] This can include functional, child-size materials for sweeping, mopping, pouring, cleaning, food preparation, folding, etc. The key is that these materials are *functional* (they work!) and that they represent a daily living skill they see the adults in their life do *every day*.

what limits movement: toys

At this point, it should seem rather counterproductive to limit movement in play, but there are a lot of popular baby toys that do just that. Here are ones to avoid:

 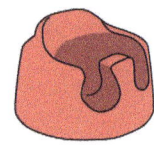  

Fitted Chairs & Activity Seats

Fitted chairs can be modular chairs for sitting or "activity saucers" where the child sits on a fabric seat with a tray of toys all around. The first and foremost problem with these is that before the child can sit, their body just isn't ready to (*it's really as simple as that!*). A sitting position for a child who is incapable of sitting is putting undue strain on the body. This is problematic because strain can lead to injury, which ultimately diverts energy away from development. In addition, fitted chairs prevent the child from adjusting their motor position (as the adult has to put them in and take them out of the chair). This lack of choice is deeply problematic to developing endurance and perseverance. As an alternative, a newly sitting child can be supported in their sitting efforts by sitting on the floor with a half-round feeding pillow around them, which simply adds a layer of cushion should they fall to one side. In this way, the child is able to build on the capacity they do have (they can sit), while being able to take a break as needed.

Jumpers & Walkers

Jumpers and walkers are contraptions that dangle the child in a seat where they can bounce or even "walk" by pushing off from their toes to move the saucer forward. Like the fitted chairs, these put undue strain on the body by putting the child into a position they aren't ready to be in. Moreover, these contraptions restrict the child's current movements (they cannot crawl or pull to stand in them), which is what they need to practice in order to walk or jump. And if that weren't enough, by introducing motor skills that are *many* months away, the child learns to be bored and frustrated with what they can currently do. This goes *completely* counter to developing perseverance. On the other hand, by letting them discover walking and jumping when they actually can walk and jump, they make this exciting leap themselves and build self-confidence instead.

Screens for Entertainment

Remember that learning is a byproduct of movement, right? Right. My body pushes a bell, my brain registers the sound, my brain tells my body to ring it again, and I learn how to make the bell ring. But what does the child's body look like when watching a screen? Well, it typically *stops* moving. This means that the child's mind is being stimulated, but their body isn't responding. It is this disconnect of the mind from its body that is counterproductive to learning itself. When this happens, the child develops unnecessary frustration when the mind tries to tell the body to do something and the body has grown accustomed to not responding.

Interactive Screens

Games (which offer some level of movement through interactivity) are problematic for a different, but important reason: the child is interacting with a virtual world that they don't know isn't real.[42] Imagine the child pushing on a screen that makes ripples appear wherever the screen  is pressed. This experience has the appearance of interacting with water, and yet the child's finger is not wet and the surface itself is hard and impenetrable. A child under the age of three simply accepts the reality we present to them (walls are hard, water is wet, pears taste like pears). If we introduce exceedingly convincing visuals that indicate a different reality (people can fly, toys come to life, water is not wet), the child will have trouble differentiating between fact and fiction, truth and lies, and reality and fantasy. This is a fractured foundation for a child who seeks to build real skills in a real world.

But . . . Don't Modern Kids *Need* Screens?

Later success with technology will not hinge on mastering what is currently available (as that will be outdated). Success will stem from knowing how to learn and the only way to "teach" that is to let the child teach themselves.[43] This means hands-on experiences where the child can experiment, estimate, and problem-solve themselves. So, while you might be thinking that children nowadays need technology to thrive in the modern world,[44] evolution doesn't work that fast. What supports human development in the first six years of life continues to be hands-on, sensorial experiences (but please check back in a couple million years for any updates on this!).

what limits movement: daily essentials

The last of our movement limiters fall into the category of daily essentials. These are items we may not be able to stop using entirely, but we can be mindful of the time the child spends in them. More to the point, however, is the time we should stop using them altogether, something I call a "developmental

birth   1 *mo*   2 *mo*

the "out of the car" car seat

Clearly, a car seat is a safety essential when using a car. However, many car seats are carted around and used well after the car is parked. This extended use of a car seat starts to impede the child's movement as they remain strapped into it well beyond its intended use. For this reason, the developmental expiration date of keeping the baby strapped into a car seat outside of the car is at birth.

the swaddle

From a motor-development perspective, swaddles are entirely counterproductive (they limit movement far beyond what the child experienced in the womb, where they could kick and suck on their fingers). From a newborn sleep perspective, however, swaddles may be helpful. While the safety end date is often around 4 months, the child may start "breaking out" of the swaddle much earlier (often around 6–8 weeks postpartum). Update accordingly and they just might find their fingers.

expiration date." This is the point at which these daily essentials increasingly start to impede the child's development, despite being considered "safe" to use. This is especially true with movement. Remember, movement is learning so it is critical to examine when our daily essentials have crossed over into restricting the child's natural development of movement so that we can limit (or eliminate) their use. Let's take a look.

3 *mo*   6 *mo*   9 *mo*   12 *mo*

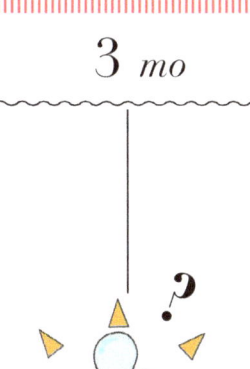

the wake-time pacifier

Pacifiers are common and have been around for ages, but there is a very different use of a pacifier as a sleep aid and one that is used to pacify an awake child. In that use, the child's communication attempts are muted. As the pacifier is often used for the sake of the adult, the developmental expiration date would be as soon as the adult feels stable after postpartum (or earlier if possible!).

carrying the walking child

The child can walk . . . when they can walk (capacity, right?). Too often, however, we continue carrying the child in strollers or carriers well after they have this capacity.[45] By doing this, the child loses out on practicing the very skill we want them to have! Once the child is walking well, leave the stroller or carrier at home and try having the child walk. Extended distance walks (3+ miles) or fast-paced walks (with a dog, for example) may be an exception for a while. Remember, they are only as capable as you allow them to be.

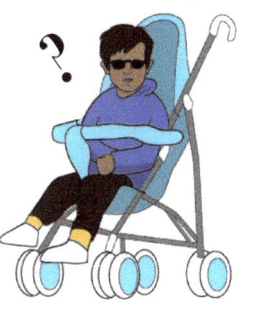

movement & the budding toddler

In the first year of life, the child was mostly limited by their own capacity. By the time the child can walk, however, their systems have mostly come "online," and they want to start using all of the skills they've built: *"What can my body do? What am I capable of? How far can I go and how fast can I get there?"* In all of this excitement, they start to push the boundaries of what we would consider appropriate behavior. Clearly defined limits to unsafe behavior will help the child successfully navigate their world. But what exactly are these "limits"?

no harm

"You can't hurt people, including yourself."

It is reasonable to stop a child's activity if they're hurting someone.

no damage

"You can't break things (even if they're yours)"

It is reasonable to stop a child's activity if they are breaking something.

no disruption

"Screaming is for emergencies only."

It is reasonable to stop a child from screaming if there is no emergency.

Limits

Limits operate best when the child feels as though they just "bumped into a wall." The wall is not angry at the child for bumping into it, and walls don't have to remember to be there every time they are needed. Walls offer a clear, consistent, and *neutral* stopping point where the child cannot continue their activity. To create this "wall," limits must first be consistently enforced (if you say, *"Don't bang on the window,"* you can't let them continue banging on the window and expect the child to understand "no banging" as a rule). Secondly, the adult's attitude in limit-setting should be as neutral as possible so that the child feels that it is their behavior that you dislike, not them. This makes it possible for the child to not feel glued to the wall, which allows them to feel like they can make a different choice next time. Neutrality is *critical* in limit-setting; it is hardly an incentive to adjust to more socially positive behavior if you are socially ostracized for your mistakes.

Setting Limits: Putting Theory into Practice

So, we know the kinds of things we want to stop, but how exactly do we stop them? First, make sure you are modeling what you want to see and refrain from modeling what you don't (they really are *always* paying attention). And the second goes like this: *"Short and sweet, rinse and repeat!"*

"Short and Sweet . . .

Limits work best when they are only a few words (short) and quickly shift into a "positive redirection" of what the child could do instead (sweet). Now, a positive redirection is not a distraction *("Look over here!")* as distractions simply ignore the behavior. Positive redirections, on the other hand, address the behavior by showing the appropriate version *("Here is something you can bang!")*. And although it may feel intuitive to use a cheerful tone in limit-setting, it's more effective to have a serious tone when saying "stop," and to switch to a more cheerful tone for the redirection. This gives the feeling of "bumping" into the wall.

. . . Rinse and Repeat!"

Consistency is best when defining a "wall," right? Right. This means you can predictably go into toddlerhood expecting to repeat yourself. For example, the child who bangs on the window will invariably bang on the exact same window right after you told them to stop. No, they are not trying to make your blood boil, they actually don't know what the rule is. You see, *you* think you are being very clear, but the young toddler doesn't yet have a concept of what the word "window" encompasses. What they heard was to not bang on one part of the window, but what about this one? The toddler has not yet built the generalized idea of what a "window" is. Only then (around 3 years old) can they have a sense that the general rule is not to bang on any part of one. So, just as a nine-month-old child will learn not to bite the breast simply because they didn't get milk when they did, limits are best "taught" by allowing the child to experience the logical consequence of their own actions (banging = no more window). When a consequence is not logical (a favorite toy is taken for banging the window), you lose your neutrality and turn consequences into punishments.[46] Punishments are problematic because they target the child instead of the behavior. Logical consequences, therefore, are ideal.

movement summary

support

give them time

let them practice

support their interests

prepare

less is *more*

give things a place and a purpose

make things visible

inspire

look up (0–6 months)

explore (6–12 months)

involve (12–18 months)

avoid

fitted chairs and activity seats

jumpers and walkers

screens

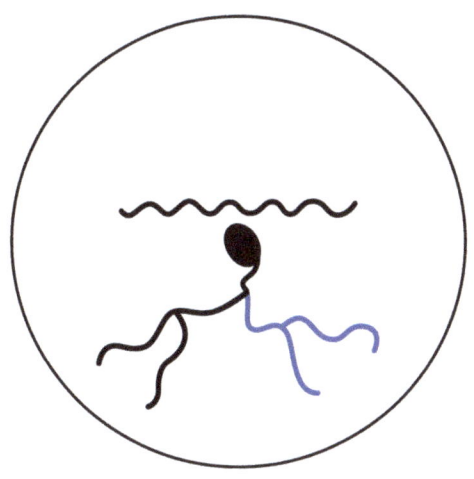

language:

the second root

illustrations by:

esma bošnjaković

why language matters

The second root of development is language. Like movement, *time*, *practice*, and *interest* are all essential components for the development of language. Time is about having the hearing apparatus and vocal cords develop and a reminder that each child's timeline is unique. Practice is about hearing an abundance of the same sounds in context so that the child can pick up on how to say things (and what they mean). Practice is also a reminder that it is only through active experience that the child becomes capable (capacity). Interest, however, will be this chapter's focus as the infant's interest in language is not exactly for socializing, it's for self-care. Let me explain.

When the child was in the womb, all of their needs were met without them having to lift a finger. At birth, one of the many startling realities is that not only do they need to begin doing things themselves (eating, breathing, eliminating), but that they need to communicate every time they are hungry, tired, wet, cold, lonely, or bored. Language becomes the essential vehicle through which they meet their own needs and enhances their understanding of their world.[47]

Supporting Language Development

The child's motivation for communicating better is that in being clearer, they will have their needs met more accurately (and more quickly). Therefore, although speaking to the child is clearly an important part of supporting language development, it is not the entirety of it. The child also needs the opportunity to figure out what they need and then be empowered to communicate what those needs are. This is the motivation that inspires more language.

Being Heard

If we simply intend to quiet or pacify the infant without finding out what they are trying to say, we miss an important opportunity when the child *could have* had the powerful experience of being heard.[48] It is when the child feels heard (not silenced) that they are inspired to talk more. Your job, therefore, is not to stop the child from crying. After all, crying is a form of communication. It would hardly support language development to stop communication. Instead, your job is to figure out what the child is trying to say (*"I'm hungry/wet/tired/bored"*) and then, to respond to meet that need. It is in this context that we will consider what supports the development of language during infancy. Let's take a look:

setting the space to inspire language

As with movement, there is an overwhelming amount of information available about language development. To get through it, it's best to understand some "big picture" ideas to guide our search for language inspiration in our spaces.

The Three Trimesters of Language

You may have noticed in the Language Timeline (see pp. 42-43) that infancy has marked transition points at six and twelve months (identical to the development of movement). These transition points play a significant role in all areas of development, and language is no exception. Around six months, the child shifts from simply using their hearing and vocal apparatuses to make sound, to using them to replicate the actual language spoken around them. You can hear this transition with the onset of "babbling," when the child repeats similar sounds *(babababa* or *mamamama)*. Later in this period, the child mixes these pairs up *(badamama)* and eventually lands on a word at around 12 months. The onset of the child's first word begins a phase called "overextension," and that initiates the last trimester of infant language.

"I don't mean exactly what I say"

The child's first words (the third trimester of language), are part of a linguistic phase where the child *overextends* the use of one word to mean many things.[50] "Apple" could mean "apple," "food in general," "round things," or even whole concepts like, "I'm hungry." This is important to recognize because while the child may appear to be communicating more clearly, they don't mean exactly what they are saying. This can lead to a number of misunderstandings between the child and the adult. Overextension is seen to fade as the child's vocabulary increases around 18 months when they have enough words to more accurately describe and understand what is being said.

more is more

With language, you get back what you put in; so the more words and exchanges the child hears, the more they will be able to say once they can talk. However, in preparing their space, books are akin to toys in the "less is more" department. Just have a few books accessible to the child (for their use) and store the rest for you to read to them.

purpose & place

Say what you mean and mean what you say. Choose your words (and your books) with a purpose. Words, stories, and visualizations play a powerful role in informing how the child understands their world and what they expect to see from it. Have a critical eye for stereotypes, bias, and non-inclusivity in your words and stories.

accessibility

Language is all around us—in conversation, in storytelling, and in everyday objects!

- **Talk to them:** Position yourself in front of them when speaking
- **Talk in front of them:** Model conversation
- **Tell stories:** Tell verbal and written stories, repeatedly
- **Position book covers outward** on the shelf so that their covers are visible

inspiring language: birth to babbling

The child in their first six months of life is not actively learning words, nor are they trying to replicate them (they are simply practicing using their ears to hear and vocal cords/tongue/lips to make sounds). The first six months are important, however, because the child is learning about the *potential* of language: to understand and be understood. Imagine yourself in a place where you didn't speak the language. Could you have your needs met? A place to stay? Someone to help you? Even without any words, you would probably still get your message across in other ways. This is because you understand that language is a tool for communication, not just a compilation of mutually understood words. This is the focus of the first six months and it is with this foundation that the upcoming expressive and receptive language developments in the next six months can flourish.

HMM...YOU DON'T SEEM HUNGRY... SHOULD WE GO OUTSIDE?

THAT'S WHAT YOU WERE SAYING! YOU WANTED TO GO OUTSIDE!

To inspire language during this time, the child needs to be engaged in a back and forth with the adult *(I ask and you provide; you offer and I accept)*. When we acknowledge the child's communication attempts *("I am heard, so I should keep speaking")* and respond to meet their needs *("Communication works! I should get better at it so it's easier to meet my needs")*, the child builds this understanding.

What Do I Say to a Baby?

More is more with language, right? Right. But between sleeping, eating, and independent playtime, there doesn't seem to be a whole lot of extra time to enrich their language, but there is! Diapering, bathing, and grooming are all times when the infant is awake, alert, and directly connected with an adult (often at eye level). Moreover, language enrichment around these hygiene tasks can offer a sensorial experience alongside the words spoken (*"This is your toe,"* as you touch their toe). This sensorial experience is essential to understanding the meaning behind the word.[51] In addition, language around hygiene tasks gives the child a better understanding of their body and its needs. When a child has a strong understanding of their body, they are able to more accurately ask for help when they need it (*"Ouch! Ankle!"* is clearly more helpful than *"Ouch! Ouch!"*). Knowing where and what your body is, is essential to identity.

engaged play

I've defined "independent play" as a time when the child entertains themselves and "engaged play" as a time when the child is entertained by the adult. A core difference in these types of play is whomever is at the center (the child or the adult). During engaged play, the child has an immersive opportunity to hear language and connect to others. When the child gets "fussy" after playing on their own for a bit, join them in play with songs, rhythmic games, and massage! This is an essential moment for language, bonding, touch, and connection.

diapering & bathing

Because diapering and bathing are great opportunities for language enrichment, it can help to make these times relaxing for *you*. Get set up ahead of time by laying out their clothes, the towel, the wipes, etc. Then, position yourself *in front of* the baby so that they can see you speaking. Lastly, tell the child what you are doing (and not how you feel about the task): *"You're wet; I'm going to take your diaper off and wipe your bottom."* By remaining warm and neutral (even when it's messy), you protect positive touch and positive associations with toileting later.

inspiring language: babbling to talking

In the first six months, the child communicated their needs—any one of the many daily necessities they were not able to do themselves. But the 6–12-month-old child now begins to meet many of these needs themselves: they start to move on their own, find and choose toys on their own, feed themselves, access sleep on their own, and even use the toilet (if given the opportunity). This surge in capacity adds something new to be communicated: *wants*.

The New Cry

The child at six months now squeals in frustration that they cannot reach their toy or cries out because they want more blueberries *right now*. If we treat these "wants" as if they were "needs," we'd rush to give them what they are asking for (no different than if a newborn were hungry). But this response has a hidden message for the child: *"I get what I want by escalating. Therefore, I should cry harder, scream louder, and kick more in order to get you to hand me the toy I can't reach."* If, on the other hand, we recognize this shift towards "wants," we have an opportunity during this formative time to teach the child that *calm* communication yields results (*"I want more blueberries. I get some when I point to them, not when I shout or bang, so I'll point to them to get more"*). This can have a profound effect on the intensity of tantrums in toddlerhood, resulting in more calm, solution-oriented communication.

The To-Do List During Frustration

As you might imagine, sorting out wants and needs takes practice and sometimes you will mix them up (and that's alright!). A good place to listen for a "want" cry vs. a "need" cry is during the child's play when the activity centers around interests (wants), not survival (needs). When we can identify this "want" cry, we can empower the child to decide for themselves how to deal with their frustration. This is not only a function of identity (everyone handles frustration differently), but also essential to perseverance.

real words

As babies start babbling and producing sounds closer to what the word sounds like ("baba" for bottle, for example), it can be tempting to replicate what they say ("*Do you want your baba?*") instead of the real, accurate word (bottle). In order to know what to say later, the child needs to hear the full, real word in the first place. This produces more usable language later (which will yield more capacity). Some of the best times for real words are at mealtimes, when conversations are hopefully audible, as well as moments for hygiene and body care.

books

The new upright posture of the sitting child makes books a lot more accessible. Books are a fantastic resource for storytelling, vocabulary enrichment and learning about a diverse set of ideas, experiences, and voices. To make book reading a frequent occurrence in your household, try adding books into a routine (so the child comes to expect them at a certain time). You can also engage a sitting child by inviting them to start turning the pages. In one hand, hold down all of the pages except the next one. Once they turn that page, continue the story.

inspiring language: talking to 18 months

The child's first words open some real doors to clearer communication, but we must remember that they don't say exactly what they mean, and they don't hear exactly what we say ("overextension"). For example, let's say your child points to a banana and says "nana." You give them a banana and instead of graciously accepting it, the young toddler throws it on the floor and starts to pitch a real fit. You might be inclined to think that they are "changing their mind," being "willful," "stubborn," or a "picky eater." However, if we know to expect overextension, we can question what we *think* we understand and take the time to really listen.

Really Listening

In the above example, let's consider that instead of trying to say, *"I want a banana,"* the child was simply identifying a banana. After all, identification of the environment is a new big skill! Children tend toward saying nouns first[52] (ball, cat, mama, dog) and then start adding words to the noun (yellow, big, go, up, more, etc.). Naming things around them is a game a child of this age loves to play *("Car! Hat! Dog! Banana!")*.
So for a child who found the bananas and correctly identified them, it might be disturbing if, instead of sharing in their excitement *("Yes, that is a banana!")*, you take them away, and might even cut them into pieces (how dare you?!).

Now, this is not to say that it's your job to ensure your child has clear communication; it's still the child's job to move out of overextension by increasing their vocabulary enough to say "this banana" or "want banana," so that they are better understood. Rather, your job is to offer them vocabulary that will help them better articulate their needs and to warmly remark that their word choice isn't clear. Here are two sample responses that do both:

> *"Yes, that is a banana. Did you want a banana? Great! Here is a banana."*
> *"Hmm, when you say banana and point to the toast, I get confused. This is called "toast." You can say "toast" when you want toast."*

The child might not say the words yet, but what you are providing is a framework of how this works: the clearer one is, the more accurately their needs will be met.

name the experience

Imagine three dogs.[53] The first is a real dog that needs food and water; it is warm, lively, and you can reach out and touch it. The second dog is a figurine that is cold, hard, immobile, and while you can touch it, it doesn't need to be fed or exercised. The third dog is a picture in a book. This dog is flat, unmoving, and does not need care and attention. If we label each of these as "dog," the child will have some serious misunderstandings about what a "dog" is. By using the language of their experience *("This is a* picture *of a dog")*, we equip them with authentic understanding.

essential vocabulary

The child this age can learn many words in a short amount of time (even if they are just understanding them and can't say them yet). It is helpful to focus your vocabulary enrichment efforts on the words that will help them better meet their needs. Yes, it's nice if they know "giraffe" and "firetruck," but essential vocabulary words will help them meet (and understand) their needs more easily (which facilitates the capacity to meet those needs). Essential vocabulary words include everyday objects, everyday food, everyday clothing and parts of the body.

what limits language

As you can imagine, the primary limit to language development is preventing communication, as communication helps the child express their needs. If the child is prevented from communicating their needs, is unaware of their needs, or (later) doesn't have the words to tell us about those needs, we lose out on an important opportunity to support their language development. So, let's take a look at a few (completely avoidable) language limiters.

Lack of Language

What the child hears, they have the potential to speak. A person can have functioning ears, tongue, vocal cords, and mind, but if they never hear language in the first six years, they actually lose the capacity to develop one. This is why the first six years is considered a "sensitive period" of language.[54] On the other hand, if you develop at least one language in the first six years, you will be able to add additional languages because you built the basic foundations of the first one(s) in the initial six years. One of the biggest language limiters, therefore, is not hearing it in the first place. So, talk to your baby!

Wake-Time Pacifier

Some babies are soothed by sucking, and pacifiers can be a helpful sleep tool before the child develops the motor skills to meet this need themselves. But this use of pacifiers is quite different in its intention than pacifiers used when the child is awake. When the child is awake, the purpose of the pacifier is to "pacify" or otherwise calm or quiet the baby. As such, the baby isn't free to tell us what they need. They could have soiled their diaper and not told us because they were soothed by the pacifier, which lessens the back and forth between the child and the adult. This back and forth is not only essential for bonding, but it is a template for conversations (someone says something and waits for a response; the other person responds). The only exception I would make for wake-time pacifier use would be for an especially colicky baby during the first 6–8 weeks, and this would be for the sanity of the adult. If you are clear with yourself about your intention *("This is for me, not for the child")*, you may be more likely to proactively phase it out for the child's sake.

Early Adult-Imposed Schedules

Some books/experts/parents advocate scheduling the baby from the start or sometime in the first three months because of the wonders of order and predictability, for both child and parent. After all, predictability and order are very important to the young child and can add stability to a time that feels very unstable for everyone. But, when the adult sets a schedule with no input from the child, the child lives a passive life without needing to communicate their needs, just like in the womb. *"I eat when it's food time, not when I communicate I'm hungry,"* or *"I sleep when it's sleep time, not when I communicate I'm tired."* This passivity not only limits the foundation of language as a vehicle to meet one's needs, but the child ends up learning to listen to *you* to meet their needs instead of learning to listen to themselves. Not knowing what their body is saying is an impediment to toilet learning, self-regulation, healthy eating habits and more. Having said all this, it does not mean that babies should have no schedule—to not give any predictability in the day can be crazy-making for the parent and the baby. The key is that the schedule is developmentally-informed (when "schedules" show up naturally in development) and that the schedule of the day is based on the child's cues (their communication). We will get into more about scheduling in the sleep chapter, but don't skip ahead! The content of the next few chapters directly informs sleep strategies. Hold tight!

Multimedia Language

The thing about language acquisition is that the child needs more than just words to absorb the language they are hearing; the child needs facial expressions, body language, and the movement of the lips and tongue (which is why it's more effective to face the baby when talking to them, instead of talking to the back of their head). This means that multimedia sources for language—recordings, radio, TV, etc.—are ineffective at providing language for the child, simply because the child isn't getting all of the requisite information. Additionally, the language presented in multimedia platforms is largely unresponsive to the child's communication attempts. For instance, the TV or radio does not slow down or repeat a word that appeared to be interesting to the child—a response that is intuitive to an interactive adult and very effective at strengthening language acquisition. Though phone or video calls may be interactive, face-to-face dialogue is much more effective.[55]

language & the budding toddler

I've talked a fair amount about this period of overextension; where the child "overextends" a single word to mean many things. But I'd like to offer another way to look at overextension, as a "partial understanding": the child has a little bit of information, but not the whole picture. From this perspective, overextension isn't a "phase," but rather a lifelong process of expanding our understanding of the world (and the people in it). So, let's take a look at an example.

In this book, I have used a banana as an example on a number of occasions. When referenced, you've likely conjured up a very specific image of a "banana" in your mind (possibly this one on the left that I showed you earlier). This is a good reminder that images are powerful, and it highlights that we are operating under an assumption that this particular image of a banana is an accurate representation of bananas in general. *But is it?* After all, there are many kinds of bananas (from yellow to red, big to small), all in various stages of ripeness that change the color, shape, texture, and taste.

If the child is presented with just one kind of banana when they are building their definitions, they are likely to build their whole definition as that specific representation of a banana. And when they encounter a different kind of banana later, it will appear as "outside" of that definition or group: "foreign," "other," or not "normal." All of these feelings are predictable, but they create a rocky foundation for bias, stereotyping, and xenophobia. If instead, the child is exposed to a lot of experiences with all kinds of bananas, they would accept this very broad understanding that some bananas are different colors, some bananas taste better than others, some bananas are big and others are small, but they are all "bananas."

This Isn't About Bananas

Of course, the point of all this is not about bananas, but about people. We have a powerful opportunity during the development of language to intentionally expand the child's definitions as they build them. Remember, the child learns language (and its definitions) by simply absorbing what is spoken around them and then by making connections with those words and the associated objects, ideas, or people. Repeated experiences with the same connections create a definition in their mind *(I hear "banana" enough times with just that one specific fruit and I stop overextending "banana" to mean anything more than a "banana")*.

But, what about the words "firefighter," "teacher," "mother," "family," "good," or even "bad"? What do these words mean? What object, idea, or person is the child connecting to repeatedly to create the definitions of these words? And how can we disrupt the repeated connections that reinforce white supremacy, anti-Blackness, sexism, misogyny, homophobia, etc.? Well, let's take a look.

Shift the Saturation Point

From the systemic roots of racism and its inherited privilege for white people (myself included), there is a saturation of visible whiteness (white leaders, white teachers, white authors, white illustrators, white characters, white spokespeople, etc.) that subtly (and not so subtly) makes white appear "normal," "standard," and by extension, "better." And, as it turns out, these biases show up just after the child's definition-building years: at around three years old, when preschoolers start showing prejudice and discrimination.[56] Therefore, a critical time to shift the saturation point is before age three. There are incredible leaders, teachers, authors, illustrators, characters, and spokespeople who are, among many other things, Black, Indigenous, and of the Global Majority. Seek out their voices by intentionally selecting books that share *joyful stories* (not ones of oppression or hard history at this age) that celebrate *everyday life* with characters of all backgrounds. Name whiteness when you see it: *"Hmm, this fire engine set only came with white firefighters. Let's ask the company for the rest of the set!"* Find non-main characters of color in books and refer to them as "the doctor" or "the president." And lastly, love the words "black" and "brown" and celebrate them regularly.

language summary

support

give them time

let them practice

listen to what they are saying

prepare

more is *more*

use real words

make language everywhere

inspire

talk during hygiene (0–6 months)

talk during meals (6–12 months)

essential words (12–18 months)

avoid

wake-time pacifiers

early adult-imposed schedules

multimedia language

the conditions:

what the child needs to grow

illustrations by:

alisha nicole brumfield   tracy nishimura bishop   brenda brambila

introduction to the conditions

Welcome to the conditions! Here you will ground yourself on the conditions that enable the child to grow: eating, sleeping, and hygiene. Each section will follow this basic outline:
- Why this essential condition matters
- The timeline of relevant developments for this condition
- Setting up the space for the transfer of this condition from the adult to child
- What limits the transfer of this condition from the adult to the child
- This condition and the budding toddler

Quick Reminders About "the Conditions":
- **The Conditions**: These are the essential conditions that support development.
- **Role of the Adult**: These are things that the adult does for the child until the child can do them for themselves. This means that there is a "transfer."
- **Activities and Materials**: These are things we use to foster the child's ability to do things themselves. For example, let's say you get a child-size infant spoon for the child to feed themselves, but they keep dropping whatever you give them. By offering something that will stay on the spoon (like mashed sweet potato), the food choice is more important than the spoon is, because it is helping support the child's ability to self-feed (capacity).

Timelines:

I will outline the developments relevant to each of these conditions in a growing timeline, as I did for the roots. As always, these are general timelines based on due date (not birth date). If you have questions or concerns about your child's development, you should consult your child's medical provider. In the timelines, we will follow the transfer from the adult taking care of this need for the child (noted in red), to the child and the adult working together to meet this need (noted in yellow), to the child meeting much of this need for themselves (noted in green). It will look something like this:

	birth	6 mo	12 mo	18 mo
Nutrition	Adult meets child's food needs	Adult and child meet child's food needs	Child meets their own food needs	

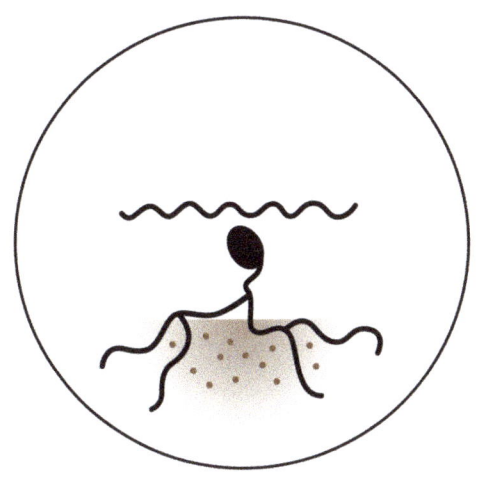

eating:

the fuel

illustrations by:

alisha nicole brumfield

why eating matters

Eating is one of the essential conditions for development (the fuel), and around 6 months the child's fuel requirements change. You see, prior to this moment, our digestive systems (like all mammals) are too immature to process the food of the environment and so we have this "special food" (breast milk or formula) packed with the nutrients young bodies need. But by around 6 months, we start needing additional nutrients, and our bodies change to accommodate this:[57] digestive enzymes are present, we lose the tongue thrust reflex (a survival mechanism to push out anything solid that is in the mouth), teeth start coming in, and our bodies position themselves by sitting to eat solid food. By around 12 months, our systems are so mature that we are able to access most of our nutritional needs directly from the food in our environment. Take a look at the timeline to see how this unfolds.

In thinking about this transfer, it might seem as though the food was the focus (shifting from breast milk/formula to "table food"). However, what is being transferred is the *responsibility* for meeting this need. It is the timely shift to table food that creates the opportunity for this transfer because the child's newly grasping hands can start to feed themselves. But despite these new capacities, there is something that can get lost in this transfer that shouldn't: *eating* by themselves doesn't have to mean *being* by themselves.

Relevant Developments for the Eating Transfer (0–18 Mo)

	birth	1 *mo*	2 *mo*	3 *mo*	4 *mo*	6 *mo*	7 *mo*
Gross Motor (Myelination)		Holds head (neck)		Rolls (shoulders)		Sits (torso)	
Fine Motor	Reflexive grasping			Voluntary grasping		Whole hand grasp	
Receptive Language			Turns head towards sounds			Begins to understand and responds	
Expressive Language			Smiles and coos			Babbling (canonical) *"the new cry"*	
Nutrition	Nutrients from breast milk or formula					New nutritional needs	
Teeth[59]						Central incisors	
Digestion	Immature digestion/tongue thrust reflex[60]					Digestive maturity	

The Social-Cultural Side of Mealtimes

When we take a look at the intersection of developmental timelines beyond the advances directly related to eating, we see that it is not just digestion and motor skills that are maturing. Language has a significant transition at around six months, especially in receptive language (understanding). This shift means that the child is "tuning in" to the actual words spoken around them and the unspoken social relationships they have with others[58] *("Am I part of this meal or not?")*. Humans are social creatures, and a lot of social-cultural connection is deeply rooted to food. No matter what the occasion, be it happy or sad, celebratory or mundane, food is always a central feature. After all, we are mammals and so every food experience in the first six months is *with* another person. Unfortunately, what often happens as the child begins table food is that this social experience becomes underdeveloped: their high chairs are often separate from the family table, their mealtimes often don't overlap with anyone else's, and their whole eating process rarely looks anything like the rest of their family's (the tools they use, the space they use, and the food they eat). It's no wonder parents often struggle with antisocial eating habits in toddlerhood: picky eating, can't stay at the table, or playing around with their utensils. Not only is the shift to table food an opportunity for the child to begin meeting their nourishment needs themselves, but if they are at a table where people are modeling social norms and conversation in addition to eating the same foods and with the same cultural tools, they are primed to absorb the fullness of the eating experience that we as adults cherish so deeply. Take a look again at how these developments intersect around six months:

8 mo	9 mo	10 mo	11 mo	12 mo	14 mo	16 mo	18 mo
Crawls (upper legs)			Stands/cruises (lower legs)		Walks (Feet)		
Thumb/fingers opposition		Pincer grasp/claps			Hand as a tool of the mind		
Knows name		Surge in understanding/ responds to simple request			Understands up to 50 words (& overextension)		
		Babbling (variegated)/points			Responds to simple request		
	(Increasingly eats food of the environment)				Nutrients mainly from environment		
	(6–12 Mo)	Lateral incisors (9–16 Mo)			First molars/canines (13–23 Mo)		

setting the space for the eating transfer

The basic premise of setting up the space for this transfer of responsibility is to get tools that will function well for the child (so that they can self-feed successfully) and to bring them into the social-cultural side of mealtimes. As luck would have it, the kinds of tools and spaces that support the child's independence with self-feeding are exactly the things that make them feel included in the first place.

The Tray-less Adjustable High Chair

Our first step toward self-feeding at the family table is to create a space for them at that table (this functions as the literal invitation to the family meal). And while it's more common to have a high chair off to the side with a tray that blocks the child from being at the table, there is another option. Tray-less adjustable high chairs come directly up to the table and have two ledges that adjust as the child grows (one for sitting and the other for the child's feet to rest). These ledges not only add comfort for the child (as dangled legs get tired), but they support the walking child's independence, as the ledges function like a ladder in toddlerhood.

Functional, Child-Size Tools

The second step in balancing the independence of self-feeding with inclusion in the family meal is with the tools the child uses. It may be all well and good that the child is at the family table, but if everything the child uses to eat with looks different than everyone else's, they will still see their mealtimes as "separate" and "different." This is not only a precursor to picky eating, but it is also a form of social exclusion from the meal. If instead, we aim to give tools that look like everyone else's, they see themselves as part of this greater social experience. Below are child-size versions of some common tools on *some* tables, but remember that food tools are *cultural*. What the child uses should match what *your* family uses, just smaller.

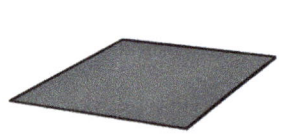
a place mat
(a plastic cutting board)

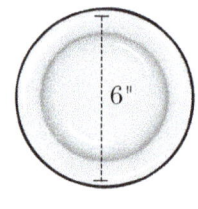
a small plate
(a bread & butter plate)

short-handled utensils
(a cake fork or "tea" spoon)

a small, open cup
(a condiment cup)

a community to eat with

The final step in setting the child up for success with this transfer is to have people for the child to eat *with*. After all, we can have the child at the family table, give them tools that they can use that look like everyone else's, but if they aren't actually sharing a meal with anyone, it's not exactly the social-cultural experience we are hoping for. And to remind you of how enjoyable these mealtimes can be, imagine the kind of "pleasant meal" you might enjoy after the baby goes to bed or when you reconnect with a few friends. What makes that time so enjoyable and coveted? Everything that you love about that meal is *exactly* what we want the child to be immersed in: conversation, connection, and presence over a meal. And when you introduce self-feeding in a way that helps the child develop capacity (by starting at the beginning of solids with functional, child-size tools) and an understanding of social norms (by modeling and limit-setting), the child ends up with the very skills they need to be pleasant company at mealtime. So, give them a seat at the family table by eating alongside them, right from the start, as much as you can.

"i do it for you" (birth to 6 months)

What marks this time is not just that they eat a "special food," but that the child is relying on us to meet their nutritional needs. Bonding and language, therefore, are mealtime essentials in these first six months of life. And to make the most of these mealtime moments, it is helpful to know what exactly they're eating.

What the Baby is Eating

Let me start with the obvious, babies need food. Although breast milk has significant benefits for both mom and baby, it is not always possible or desirable for all parents. Fed really is best! So, what are they eating?

Colostrum[61] **(birth to 3ish days)** is the baby's first "milk." It is low in fat (which eases digestion) and high in antibodies (which protects from illness).

Breast milk[61] **(3ish days +)** is the milk that "comes in" 3–5 days postpartum. This milk is high in fat (needed for myelin) and antibodies (which protect from illness). Although there is just one milk, the fat may be more concentrated when the breast is relatively empty, because the fat sticks to the milk-making cells at the back of the breast (this is often called "hindmilk").[62] When the breast is full, the milk (often called "foremilk") may be less fatty. Offering a "full feed" on one side before moving to the next is recommended for a full-fat meal. Pro-tip: Poop color can be a helpful gauge of fat intake:

- **Green** may indicate the child isn't getting enough fat
- **Yellow** (with white specs of fat) may indicate that they are getting enough

Formula[63] is a manufactured alternative to breast milk with a nutritional profile modeled as close as possible to breast milk. Formulas do not have antibodies.

The Child's Active Experience in Feeding

While the child is relying heavily on you for their food, they *do* have an active role in feeding: communication. This is essential to the roots of both identity *("I can make choices about my body")* and language *("I am heard, so I should keep talking")*. The child is the only one who knows whether they are hungry or full. The feeding experience, therefore, is generally best when paced by the child[64] (aside from any medical condition). This may mean tipping the bottle back to "check in" and see if they really want more, offering food after signs of hunger instead of by timed intervals, or stopping the feed when they turn their head away.

breastfeeding

If the aim is to breastfeed, get support with latching early!

- **Nipples matter**: Size and shape change best feeding position.
- **There isn't just one latch.** You may need to adjust along the way, so be prepared!
- **Don't settle for a bad latch!** Bad latches are inefficient (and uncomfortable)! Take the baby off and then try again.

bottle feeding

If the aim is to bottle-feed, get support early to understand your formula and pumping options. If you aim to bottle-feed a breastfed baby, consider starting the bottle between 3–4 weeks postpartum with 1–2 ounces daily. This gives enough time for the child to learn how to latch onto the breast and not too much time before they may not take a bottle.

starting solids

Toward the end of the first six months, the child's body is getting ready for solid food to meet their growing nutritional needs. A great way to start is with tastes of natural juices[65] (like the squeezed juice from a watermelon or a cucumber). This allows the child to orient to the newness of solid food in a developmentally-accessible way (as a liquid).

"we do it together" (6 to 12 months)

While breast milk/formula is still an important part of the child's diet during this time, starting solids marks the beginning of the transfer for the child to begin nourishing themselves. As the focus of this transfer is not on the food itself, but rather on *who* is meeting this need, self-feeding plays a significant role.

Self-Feeding is Messy *(So Lean Into It!)*

You are clearly better at feeding a baby than they are. This, of course, is not the point. The only way for a baby to self-feed successfully is if the feeding part is *in their hands*.

> **the tutorial!**
> See this in action from 5–12 months at:
> thepeaceprogram.org/resources

- **Less is More:** A great way to contain the mess is to offer small portions (only give as much as you are willing to clean up). In addition to reducing the mess, small portions create an opportunity to model a back and forth that is similar to conversation *("Do you want more? . . . Here you go!")*. This will be foundational to listening skills in conversation later.
- **Practice Makes Perfect:** The root of capacity is *practice*. Every time the child has a tool in their hand instead of yours, the child is learning how to use it and what it's for (see tips on the next page about using a second spoon).
- **The Child Is Capable:** It might be surprising to think that the child can master these tools in infancy (but they really can).

Self-Feeding isn't Destructive *(So Lean Out of That!)*

Antisocial behaviors (banging, throwing, yelling, etc.) can sometimes be difficult to differentiate from good, positive exploration. Try focusing on whether what you are seeing looks *productive* to eating (the child is visibly trying to get food or water into their mouth). And if it doesn't look productive, try the following:

- **Set Limits:** Remember logical consequences? We're going to use those to guide social norms. This means that if the child is yelling for more, wait until they are calm (or at least calm*er*) to give them more. If they are banging their plate, move the plate out of reach until they stop and then return it. If they continue, it may mean they aren't hungry anymore (See Limits, pp. 38-39).
- **Less is More:** Many of the behaviors that would require limit-setting start showing up at the end of meal when they aren't that hungry anymore. Small portions help you see if the child is actually done with the meal.

6–8 months	8–10 months	10–12 months

soft food
The type of food you serve is *cultural*, not developmental (so you need not start with a specific type of food). Start slow (one food at a time) and soft (as soft foods actually stay on the spoon).

finger food
As the child's fine motor movements improve and they pick up foods with their fingers, don't forget about the spoon! Capacity with utensils will set the stage for toddler meals that aren't just finger food.

family food
When the child is able to eat a child-sized version of whatever their family is eating, this means they have had enough experience with food to use utensils and eat the variety of foods offered.

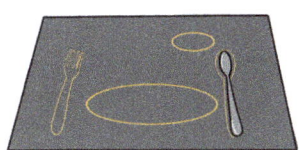  

spoon & mat
The thing about the beginning of self-feeding is that the child isn't all that good at it. Let your child have their own spoon to practice and use a second spoon to make sure they still get their meal.

plate & cup
To introduce the plate and open cup, consider how either are meant to be used: the plate stays flat and the cup is lifted only when drinking. If the child starts playing with either, briefly move them out of reach.

fork & bowl
Once the child is capable of using the spoon, they may be ready to start using a fork. Watch for when your child tries to poke their food with the spoon as this often means that a fork would be useful!

"you do it yourself" (12 to 18 months)

Separations and attachments are bittersweet and inevitable parts of life that are deeply intertwined. When we separate from something, we also attach to something else. It is this nuance that allows us to embrace an upcoming separation by celebrating the new attachment.[66] Weaning (when the need for the special food lessens) is one of those separations that is often* part of this time period as the self-feeding child begins to more completely nourish themselves.

All the Feels

Parents have very specific feelings about the weaning process because feeding is often the first attachment after the separation of birth (so it's a big deal to separate from that initial attachment). It can be helpful to remember that the separation of birth gave way to this celebrated attachment of meeting the child! So, too, does the separation from "special food" give way to the celebrated attachment of the child connecting to their community and their culture, right from the family table.

Supporting Separation

If the child is bottle-feeding, they typically have the motor skills to use a cup from 12 months of age and as such, can drink any liquid (formula, milk, or water) from a cup with no need for a bottle. A helpful gauge as to whether the child is still interested in breastfeeding or not is to feed them when they request it, not necessarily out of habit or routine. In addition, as the child eats more solid food, it is important to offer water regularly so that the child is properly hydrated.

Supporting Attachment

As noted, the attachment to community is cause for celebration as the child is eating the food of their community and can engage more fully in these social-cultural moments. Their new expressive language skills allow for real conversation, and their ability to walk allows them to fully participate in mealtimes. Once walking, the child can start to set the table, prepare food, and even climb into and out of their adjustable high chair. This participation sets the child up to be a collaborator in taking care of others—a tremendous foundation for their social development later.[67]

---

* Often, not always! The World Health Organization promotes breast feeding through at least two years of age. This is especially applicable if the nutrients available in the environment are insufficient for growth.[68]

preparing the space

In order for the child to set a table, prepare food, or clean up after mealtimes, they need materials that are accessible to them. Consider adjusting a low shelf in the kitchen to house materials for the child—cups, plates, utensils, place mats, sponges, or table crumbers. This not only allows the child to take out and put away these mealtime essentials, but it allows them to take responsibility for the tasks that need to be done, which include cleaning up. When the child takes ownership of their space (and their mistakes), they create invaluable skills for building friendships later.

preparing the meal

The refinements of the hand (and extensive practice with utensils from 6–12 months) lead the child to be more successful with meal preparation tools. Some great additions include wavy choppers, small spatulas, small cutting boards, short-handled spreaders, and a small apron. Try arranging needed tools on a tray (for jam spreading, it may be a plate with a cracker, a spreader, and a small bowl with jam); then, show them how it's used by silently and slowly (see, pp. 10) spreading the jam on a cracker. Pro tip: they want to do what you *do*, not what you *say*.

what limits self-feeding

At this point it should seem rather counterproductive to continue feeding the baby when they are (mostly) capable of feeding themselves, but even with deliberate efforts to support this, there are some materials in our spaces that might limit success. The good news is that they're avoidable.

The Tray

There are several challenges with high chairs that have trays. The first is probably the most obvious, as it separates the child from the table. This is the first of many clues the child receives that their eating experience is different than everyone else's, which weakens the root of capacity for participating in those mealtimes later. But the other challenge with the tray is that because of its lightweight and moveable nature, eating tools often don't sit well on them. Because of this, plates and open cups are often removed from the child's place setting, which is the second clue the child receives: *"my tools don't match yours."* Furthermore, at walking, the child has the potential to climb into and out of their chair but can't because the tray is in the way! This perpetuates a dependence on the adult for the child to join the meal.

"Kid" Tools

We often give children utensils that are far too big for their hands (or mouth) and as such, we see far less capacity than they actually have! After all, tools help us do more with our hands. They allow us to wield more strength than our hands or body have and allow for more nuanced motions (like bringing soup to our mouths). But when tools are the wrong size, they mask capacity instead of generating it. For example, you might feel quite capable of using a fork to pick up noodles. Imagine that instead of a standard fork, I gave you an oversized serving fork. All of a sudden, you would struggle with something that otherwise, you are most certainly capable of doing! Tools that fit *the child's hands* give us a much better sense of their actual capacity, which allows us to step back when they can do it themselves.

Lack of Modeling

Remember the absorbent mind (see p. 9)? The child is absorbing everything effortlessly all of the time. Well, one of the best ways to show the child how to use utensils is by simply using them yourself. Yes, it is more effective for an infant to watch you feed yourself than it is to "teach" a child how to feed themselves by doing it for them. In addition, if the child is with adults who are having conversation with each other, the child is learning how conversations work! This gives the child the opportunity to establish themselves as a person who is capable of taking care of themselves (identity) within the context of their social community. The ability to both meet your own needs and participate in community is essential to feeling connected to the group (a feeling necessary to follow social rules).

"But, Won't My Child Self-Feed Eventually?

At this point you might be wondering if you can cover the "social-cultural" side of mealtimes with everything except the self-feeding part. What should it matter who is feeding the child as long as they are included in the family meal? Besides, they won't need to be fed forever, right? Well, for starters, *babies* build toddlers, remember? That means that the fundamental roots that allow the child to be capable *later* are built in infancy. Plus, if the child can use utensils when they reach toddlerhood, they actually have better access to these social-cultural experiences.

Imagine that you've just walked into a fancy restaurant where your place setting has eight spoons, eight forks, and eight knives, each with its own predetermined purpose. In this situation, are you immersing yourself in the conversation? Are you connecting with the people around you? No! You're too distracted by the

utensils you don't know how to use! *This* is the toddler who hasn't already learned to use utensils. By not knowing how to use these very basic tools for eating, they are not actually focusing on the social-cultural side of the mealtime, even when they're there! Remember that the toddler is hyper-focused on acquiring language, and they can make the most of this development by being fully present when they are most likely to hear language. This means focusing not on *how* to be there (because they already have those skills), but on *who* is there with them.

eating & the budding toddler

Given the sheer quantity of language at mealtimes and the incredible opportunity this is during toddlerhood, our goal thus far has been to protect the child's place at the family table. And to this aim, we have worked toward having the child know how to be there and eat the same things while they're there. But that last one is where it can get a little tricky with a toddler.

Don't Fall for Picky Eating!

Frustrations that play out as tantrums are a common part of toddlerhood. Some tantrums can be attributable to order (see p. 32), others stem from a gap in language ability that makes it hard to feel understood, and some can be traced back to the emergence of the word "me" (identity). Remember that "me" is a declaration that they are their own person with their own thoughts and choices. A common place for the child to assert these thoughts and choices is right at the dinner table with "picky eating." You see, picky eating is not actually about food *preferences*; it's about food *autonomy*. This means that the child simply wants a voice in the process, and the best way to do that while balancing a healthy plate of food is by giving them choices.

Making Good Choices

To be a functional choice maker (something some adults are still working on), the child needs a reasonably limited quantity of things to choose from. The best way to give the child choices, therefore, is to put a limited number of options on their plate and then, let the child choose what to eat. Too often, fruit is held hostage until the vegetables are eaten, but this just exacerbates the problem because it restricts their choice. The basic idea here is that you are in control of the "universe of options" (what goes on the plate), but within those options, the child decides what to eat and when to eat it. Then, if the child doesn't want to eat what is in front of them, follow the one golden rule for non-picky eating:

"You don't have to eat it,
but you can't ask for more if you still have food to eat on your plate."

eating summary

support

invite them to the table
orient them to the tools
model mealtimes

prepare

a place at the table,
a community to eat with,
and functional, child-size tools

inspire

attention (0–6 months)
conversation (6–12 months)
participation (12–18 months)

avoid

trays
non-functional tools
lack of modeling or opportunity

sleep: read this *first*

Much of what Dr. Montessori noted about sleep was more about where it was happening than it was about how sleep develops or how the ability to meet this need is transferred from the adult to the child.[69] Therefore, much of the content in this section is based on my own application of the Montessori Method, whereby I studied the development of sleep, observed infant sleep patterns with the families I've worked with (and those of my two kids), and drew my own logical conclusions from those milestones. In light of this, let's freshen up on the following:

Developments Intersect

If you are reading this without having read the previous chapters, *go back*. Sleep is not the first chapter in this book for a reason. Movement, language, and eating all intersect with and develop in tandem with sleep. Understanding how these developments unfold will not only pave the way to better understand sleep development, but they will empower you to better decide what to do about it.

This Isn't a Book of Answers

I am not a sleep expert and as this is not a book of sleep solutions; this chapter will not outline a specific and universal sleep *approach*. Rather, this chapter will outline the developmental context around sleep over the course of infancy so that you can answer some of your questions yourself. My ultimate goal is to enable you to use the Montessori Method as I have done so that you can create your own approach to getting everyone the restful, restorative sleep they need.

The Montessori Method & Sleep

Here's Dr. Montessori's big idea: if we understand the development the child is trying to master and aim to support that development within our spaces and ourselves, we'll get a whole lot closer to the child's potential. And sleep is no different. This means that once you understand its development, there is a fair amount of *observation* (getting to know your baby) and *trial and error* that is expected and encouraged to support sleep the "Montessori" way.

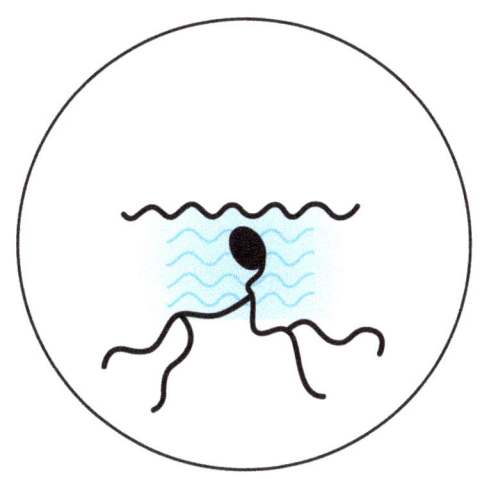

sleeping:

repair, processing & memory

illustrations by:

tracy nishimura bishop

why sleep (& a space for it) matters

Sleep is our second condition for development. During sleep, we process our experiences, store memories, and much more. It is so essential to our well-being that, without enough of it, our mood, memory, and cognitive function quickly deteriorate.[70] This transfer is going to be from the adult getting the child to sleep to the child sleeping on their own (yes, it *is* possible).

Now, "sleeping on their own" does not mean "sleeping in their own space" or "sleeping through the night without feeding." It simply means that the child has the ability to get themselves to sleep. But at this point some might argue that there shouldn't even be a transfer because if you help the child to sleep from the beginning, they develop "bad habits." Unfortunately, this fails to address the fact that the child is upset. Moreover, the child has grown accustomed to living in motion and sucking on their fingers in the womb, so *of course* they continue to ask for bouncing, rocking and suckling after birth. To not help them when they ask at this stage does not make them magically capable of self-soothing; they just simply learn to stop asking (which undermines the developments of both language and bonding). But as babies are wont to do, *they don't stay babies*. They grow and become capable (hence the transfer). So, let's set the stage for the transfer by taking a look at where sleep is happening in the first place . . .

A Space for Sleep

From cribs to bassinets, co-sleeping to co-sleepers, families have a special sleep space for their newborn. This space, however special, is nearly always oriented to the height of the adult. This matters because it can be hard to make the "sleeping on their own" transfer when the adult is the gatekeeper of the child's sleep space. So rather than using a sleep space oriented to the adult, Dr. Montessori had the not-so-revolutionary idea of simply putting the mattress on the floor[71] so that it was accessible to the child. Practically, this means that the parents can lie with the child in the *child's* sleep space to avoid the awkward transferring out of arms and can either stay with the child or go back to their adult bed to sleep. Floor beds not only ease middle-of-the-night feedings early on, but they support mobile babies in being able to get into their bed when they are tired and get out of their bed when they are rested. Sounds pretty simple—just as their space should be . . .

safety check

Typical room safety checks would include mounting furniture to the walls, plugging up outlets, and keeping the materials in the room simple and safe for the baby's exploration. The mattress itself should meet the specifications for safe infant sleep, especially in the level of firmness. Check with your medical provider for best practices.

the mattress

There are many sizes of mattress that work as a floor bed (from crib to toddler to twin). Twin mattresses, however, can be much more comfortable for the adult when lying next to the child for feeding or comforting. A lower mattress is often preferable (for the occasional roll off the bed), along with an area rug underneath for comfort and warmth.

the other stuff

Simple means *few*. You might have 3–4 safe toys and 3–4 board books (and that's it!). Dangled toys should not be in the child's space when playing independently, though an out-of-reach visual mobile over the bed can be quite pleasant. If using a feeding chair, use a stationary one to prevent explorations with the chair's rocking mechanism.

the development of the sleep transfer

Now that we have a space for sleep, let's take a look at the milestones that will be most relevant to our transfer: 6–12 weeks, 4 months, and 6+ months.

6–12 Weeks & the Production of Melatonin

Melatonin is a hormone that makes us tired when it's dark (night) and awake when it's light (day). It's like an internal clock telling our bodies when to sleep and when to wake. The problem with newborns is that their time in the womb didn't expose them to day and night, so they don't produce melatonin at first.[72] Babies can get *some* melatonin from breast milk[73] (if available), but they still need 6–12 weeks of day/night exposure to start making it themselves. This is important because it means that *before* about 6 weeks, there really isn't a schedule (so you can stop looking for one). It also means that *after* this period, the child begins to develop their own unique schedule. The sweet spot of baby scheduling is following *the child's* schedule, which means you'd have to know what it is first! Any noticeable indication of alignment to day and night after six weeks is helpful to note, most especially the appearance of consistent "wake times" between their naps. Once this appears, these wake times often become very consistent and can help you follow your child's daily rhythms (more on this later!).

Relevant Developments for the Sleeping Transfer (0–18 Mo)

	birth	1 *mo*	2 *mo*	3 *mo*	4 *mo*	6 *mo*	7 *mo*
Gross Motor *(Myelination)*		Holds head (neck)			Rolls (shoulders)	Sits (torso)	
Fine Motor	Reflexive grasping				Voluntary grasping	Whole hand grasp	
Teeth						Central incisors	
Sleep			Melatonin production		Mature sleep		
Other Milestones	Eyesight range of 7"–30"		Tracks objects		Depth/color maturation		
Sensitive Periods	Bonding & attachment* (See more in "The Gardener," p. 103)						

4 Months & the Maturation of Systems

Sleep (like most newborn systems) is immature at birth. It matures around four months[74] (which is often referred to as the "4-month sleep *regression*" despite it being a sleep *maturity*). The thing about mature sleep is that it includes routine wakeups after each sleep cycle (every 90 or so minutes overnight). And while adults mostly don't remember these wakeups, they are an important survival mechanism to "check in" with our surroundings to make sure everything looks as it did when we fell asleep (so that we aren't helplessly unconscious for eight hours). When this maturity appears, the child starts to pay attention to *where* and *how* they sleep (*"Am I in the same place?" "Now that I'm awake, how do I get back to sleep?"*). These questions are relevant to our sleep transfer because they create an often abrupt shift in the adult's role. Rocking, for example, may have been a wonderful sleep support when the child's wasn't really paying attention, but now is the source of this developmental alarm: *"Help! Something is wrong! I fell asleep in one place* (your arms), *and now I'm in another* (my bed)*!"* Sleep simply gets complicated.

6 Months & the Era of Sleep Disturbances

But that's not all! Six months marks the beginning of a period plagued by sleep disturbances (teething, separation anxiety, mobility). These repeat offenders often require *more* adult support (not less) and make it difficult to find a time free of them to transfer this skill. In the following chart, we can see the developments that need more support (red), those that require minimal support (green), and what turns out to be the *least complicated* window for this transfer, between 4–6 months (yellow):

8 *mo*	9 *mo*	10 *mo*	11 *mo*	12 *mo*	14 *mo*	16 *mo*	18 *mo*
Crawls (upper legs)			Stands/cruises (lower legs)		Walks (feet)		
Thumb/fingers opposition	Pincer grasp/claps				Hand as a tool of the mind		
	(6–12 Mo)		Lateral incisors (9–16 Mo)		First molars & canines (13–23 Mo)		
	Object permanence & separation anxiety *(Can I meet my needs?)*						
					Order (1–3 Years)		

"i do it for you" (birth to *4ish* months)

The first four months are a time when the child is typically helped to sleep by the adult. Now, while some kiddos might be happy to doze off without support; most of us are left rocking, bouncing, and shushing our way through the newborn phase. And that's alright because there are no bad habits, right? Right! But this doesn't mean we can't cultivate good ones.

The Good Habits

As an adult, you've been making melatonin since early infancy, but you don't have to go to sleep as soon as it's dark out. This is because you can override your "internal clock" that is telling you to go to bed by not "going to bed" (i.e. by changing your routines). In fact, once the child's internal clock starts ticking, they start to look at *you* for their sleep cues more than whether it's dark outside *("Is it really bedtime?")*. Not only does this allow you to weather the changes of the seasons more easily, but it also allows you to focus on the strongest social cue for sleep: routines.[75] Routines are any consistent order of events (i.e. 1. Change their diaper 2. Feed 3. Sing a song and 4. Rock to sleep). "A consistent order" means that you do the *same steps* in the *same order* before sleep. With enough consistency, the child starts to predict when sleep time is approaching and therefore, becomes more restful and ready for that final transition to sleep. Both routines and early exposure to natural light (going outside during the daytime) help facilitate the development of this internal clock.[76]

Getting Enough Sleep

The big idea here is that the child needs 11–12 hours of nighttime sleep and ever-decreasing amounts of daytime sleep over the course of the first 4–5 years (yes, I said *years*). But what exactly is "nighttime" and "daytime"? Simply put, "nighttime" is the period of 11–12 hours when the child wakes to eat and promptly goes right back to sleep. "Daytime," on the other hand, is the 11–12 hours when the child wakes for a period of time before going back to sleep ("naps"). The intervals between naps are often called "wake times." Wake times get longer as the child gets older; often starting around 45 minutes at 6 weeks and extending to roughly 2 hours around 3–4 months. Getting enough sleep means protecting the 11–12 hours of overnight sleep and, in the first six months, their 3–5 naps during the day.

0–6*ish* weeks

Routines are the first good habit as they create a predictable imprint of the steps that lead to sleep. They can start as often as you can do them and as early as you can get to them (whatever you can do is perfect, *really*). Do remember, though, that the following will mostly likely *not* be consistent: where the child sleeps, how they get to sleep, or how long they sleep.

6*ish*–12 weeks

Once the predictability of their "wake times" emerges at around six weeks, you can anticipate and follow how it changes over time. For example, if the child has a 45-minute wake time and woke at 7 a.m., look for tired queues *around* 7:45 a.m. for their first nap. If they don't look tired, it may be that their wake time has stretched 15–30 minutes.

12–16 weeks

With the upcoming 4-month sleep maturity (see notes, pp. 79), it can be helpful to note the typical timing of overnight feedings. Knowing when they typically eat (say, 12 a.m. and 3 a.m.) can help you differentiate between food-related wakeups and these developmental check-ins. This allows you to prioritize feeding for the food-related wakeups.

"we do it together" (*4ish* to 6 months)

Do you ever feel like you sleep better at home and wake up more often when you're somewhere else? Well, you wake up to do these "check-ins" no matter where you are sleeping, but the difference is that you end up waking more fully when you have to think about where you are each time. A large part of weathering the four-month sleep maturity, therefore, is about having a *consistent sleep space*.

The Where

If the child falls asleep where they will wake up *and* they sleep in the same place for the most part, the idea is that they have a better chance of not fully waking up when they check-in and will (hopefully) just go back to sleep. Of course, the more awake the child is at their check-ins, the more likely it is that they will need help getting back to sleep. Remember, this does not mean that you can get a "head start" by not helping them to sleep from the beginning—they aren't really paying attention at that age, and can't even *see* far enough to recognize where they are (see eyesight timeline, pp. 28). In the early months, use sleep supports that are working and focus your efforts on establishing a sleep routine. Then, once you notice a sustained and consistent increase in wakeups around four months, you may want to favor a single sleep space. This may mean limiting on-the-go naps, avoiding new sleep spaces at 4 a.m., or limiting travel with your child (if you can!).

The How

A consistent sleep space will be of no use to the child if they are not *awake in that space* at the onset of sleep. At this four-month transition, this means shifting from putting the child down *asleep* to putting them down *awake*, which brings us to *how* the child is getting to sleep. Whether it be rocking, bouncing, nursing, or otherwise, *this* is what the child is looking for when you put them down awake (because they, like you, would like to sleep). The question is whether they can replicate a version of that activity themselves. So, before we tackle this question, let's consider what "maturity" means within the context of development. Maturity means *independence*. When the digestive system matures, the child can feed themselves. When the body matures, the child can move themselves. And when sleep matures, the child can get to sleep themselves, too. Independence is the developmental outcome of maturity, but only if we allow the child to do these things themselves.

When Movement Leads to Sleep (or Not!)

For a child that gets to sleep with motion (rocking, bouncing, carrying, car rides, etc.), they often despise movement-limiters (like the swaddle). The motor skill of rolling (at around four months) will be significant for this child as they can finally re-create that motion for themselves. If given the opportunity, this movement-loving child may kick, rock, spin, or twist themselves to sleep. This child needs the *time* to practice their motor skills during the day and the *opportunity* to apply them at night. Do note that if your child has not shown a strong attachment to motion or has loved movement-limiters like the swaddle, it's possible that your child finds movement stimulating. This, again, is a reason to reduce adult-provided motion.

When Sucking Leads to Sleep

For a child that gets to sleep by sucking (nursing, pacifiers, etc.), they often begin to reject the once-beloved swaddle because they can't access their hands. The motor skill of grasping (at around three months) will be significant for this child as they can finally control their hands to get their fingers in their mouth (if accessible)! This may be time to remove the sleep pacifier (as the child can do this themselves now).

All the Feels

At this point, you might be wondering what to do if the child cries out when you put them down awake. First, know that there is no one-size-fits-all approach. Remember that crying is *communication,* and your job is to figure out what the child is trying to say (not to just silence them). After all, they could be saying, *"Help! I need you,"* or they could be saying, *"I'm really trying to do this!"* This is important because the former is supported by stepping *in* and the latter is supported by stepping *back*. Listen in during playtime for sounds of frustration when the *"I'm really trying to do this"* cry is more common. I'd also encourage you to ask yourself this: if your child cried at *every* diaper change, would you still change them? Yes! Just like hygiene, sleep is an essential condition. The first question to ask, therefore, is whether they are getting enough sleep. And if they aren't despite your best efforts, consider what a sage parent once told me: *"If nothing is working, it just might mean that* nothing *works."* Sometimes, a step back *is* the best step forward (and your child just might surprise you!).

"you do it yourself" (6–18 months)

This is a time marked by sleep disturbances when the child wants and needs extra sleep support because of all of the teething, separation anxiety, and sleep-disrupting motor skills the child wants to practice all day and night (see timeline, p. 79). It's important to note that the support you offer does not have to look like it did earlier in their infancy—when you were putting them to sleep. *This* support is about helping the child navigate physical pain (teething), excitement around mobility (motor milestones), and feelings of separateness (separation anxiety). Therefore, it is helpful to avoid re-introducing sleep supports like bouncing, rocking, or sucking just to help them get back to sleep. These "supports" don't really address the underlying problem (even if the child temporarily goes back to sleep) and may erode some of the independent sleep habits the child has already formed. Instead, consider the following:

teething

The hallmark of this sleep disturbance is pain. Walking into the room doesn't take the pain away, so the child is often still upset. Acute teething (when the tooth is actively cutting through the gum) is typically 24–48 hours of pain. Providing comfort and/or pain relief helps. Moreover, the floor bed allows you to lie next to the child to comfort them while still getting some rest yourself.

motor milestone

The hallmark of this sleep disturbance is movement; a child who wakes in the night to practice their new motor moves. Ultimately, part of their development is to learn how to UN-sit, UN-stand or crawl *back* onto their bed. This is something they will figure out if you let them! Give them ample time during the day to move around freely so that they can have ample time in the day to practice those skills.

separation anxiety

The hallmark of this sleep disturbance is that the child calms immediately with your presence. This can last 1–3 months and may be more of a disruption at the initial separation (bedtime) than it is overnight. Sitting with your child and providing company supports them through this period. The floor bed gives space for extra snuggles while still allowing the child to put themselves to sleep.

11–12 hours nighttime sleep

6–9 months

By about 6 months, many babies have (mostly) consolidated their daytime sleep into 2–3 naps totaling 1–3 hours. Overnight sleep is 11–12 hours, possibly without a night feeding. It may be helpful to notice whether night-feedings are at the same time every night, in which case the feedings may be more habitual than necessary.

9–12 months

At 9 months, most babies have dropped their third nap and have settled into daytime naps at more or less predictable times in the morning and afternoon. This period is often a difficult time for overnight sleep as the most common sleep disruptions overlap. Get everyone the support they need by prioritizing sleep for all over a particular approach.

12–18 months

At around 12 months, some babies begin to drop their morning nap and transition to a large midday nap of several hours (a "toddler" nap). Only having one nap indicates a 4–5 hour wake time period (7 a.m.–12 p.m., for example). If the child only has a 3–4 hour wake time period, they are not likely to be ready to drop one of their two naps.

what limits independent sleep

"Independent sleep," as you may recall, does *not* mean that the child needs to sleep in their own space, nor does it mean the child can "sleep through the night" without eating. It simply means that after the child's sleep matures, they can get themselves to sleep. And the number one thing that limits independent sleep is not observing your individual child. Perhaps *your* child will sprout teeth at 4 months of age, not 6. Or they might not roll until 6 months. Or their sleep might mature closer to 3 months of age, not 4. Therefore, you will be in a better position to support your child's sleep when you pay attention to their *individual* motor timeline, disposition, preferences, and cues. In addition, it can help to avoid the following:

The Swing

The key to independent sleep is not that sleep has to be separate from the adult, but that the child can get to sleep on their own. The swing (or any other automated rocking sleep support) is not much help in this regard because it is still assisting the child in sleep, just not with the adult's arms. If the child still needs assistance, arms at least have the benefit of physical touch (a bonding essential!). In addition, swings limit the child's ability to roll, which limits their ability to replicate motion themselves.

Not Updating Your Approach

Quality sleep for the baby and the adult is the priority. So if sleep is getting worse with more of the same, it may be time to do something different. For example, carrier or stroller naps might be great at the beginning, and then start to yield less sleep for the distractible 3–4 month-old child. Or bouncing may have gotten the baby to sleep in 10 minutes when they were two months old, and now it takes 2+ hours! Take the hint and update accordingly!

Whenever you are establishing a new routine or approach based on new developmental skills or transitions, it's best to be consistent! Establishing a better pattern for sleep, therefore, is not about exactly what you are doing, but rather how consistent you are when you do it. There are many ways to reach healthy sleep habits as long as sleep for the individual child is at the center.

sleep & the budding toddler

Have you ever heard of the terrible twos? You know what makes a toddler even more cranky? No, it's not the shoes that you put on the "wrong" shelf and it's not the snack they just refused that they desperately want now. It's not getting sufficient sleep. Ensuring that the toddler gets enough sleep is one of the best ways to support their relationship with you and their sunny disposition. The twos aren't as terrible as they are made out to be! But from incoming molars to their new toddler assertiveness, toileting awareness to that last hug and kiss goodnight, getting enough sleep may feel like a dream rather than a reality. So, what can you do?

An Accessible Bed in a Safe, Enclosed Room

What's great about starting the floor bed in infancy is that it introduces independence around the room at a time when they are far less assertive in their space. If having access to their room is new to the toddler, they will often delay sleep time given all of the excitement of their newfound freedom. Remember, the floor bed is about sleep *access*, so any arrangement where the child can get in and out of their bed themselves will suffice. An accessible bed not only reduces bedtime battles with the parent, but it gives  the child the freedom to just go back to bed when they are tired and ready. Therefore, having a baby gate (or the like) at the room door helps to support the child's explorations in leaving (and ultimately returning) to their sleep space, while also keeping them in the room.

Let Them Help!

Remember that the young toddler is still in their sensitive period of order, which means routines are of paramount importance to sleep. And for the young toddler who wants to do everything themselves, they may want to start participating in the routine itself. Let them change their clothes, brush their teeth, stand on a stool to turn out the light, pick the book, turn the pages, and choose the next song. By engaging them in the bedtime routine, they have more agency over themselves (and don't push back on you quite as much!).

sleeping summary

support

listen, instead of pacify

give them routines

notice when sleep changes

prepare

an accessible bed

in a safe, enclosed room

inspire

help them! (0–4 months)

follow where & how (4–6 months)

trust that they can (6–18 months)

avoid

swings

not updating your approach

inconsistent routines

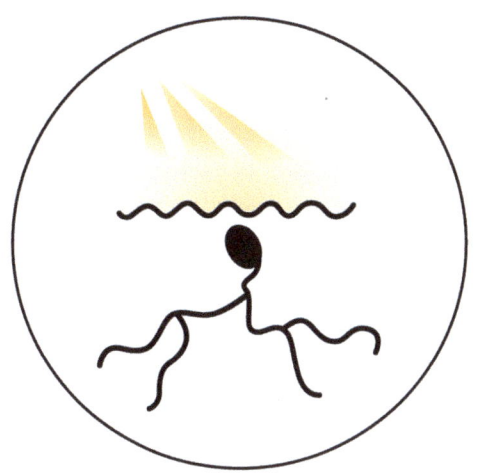

hygiene:

health & well-being

illustrations by:

brenda brambila

the development of the hygiene transfer

Hygiene is our last condition for development and includes things like grooming (hair, skin, or nail care), bathing (face and body washing) and diapers/toileting. Basically, hygiene matters because it helps us avoid illness, and fighting illness takes energy and nutrients away from development.[77] The transfer is one of responsibility for meeting these needs: from us to the child themselves. And despite this sounding pretty familiar, the hygiene transfer is a little more complicated than it was for sleeping or eating. You see, the hygiene tasks all require some sort of tool to be successful: a toilet, a sponge, a comb, a toothbrush, clothing, etc. Using tools is relevant because not only do we have to wait for the child's basic skills to develop, but we also have to wait for the child to understand what "tools" are in the first place, something they need some time to discover. Sitting, as it turns out, is an important milestone for both.

Once the child can sit, they have more functional use of their hands, which will satisfy the "basic skills" part of using tools. Moreover, sitting occurs around the time of starting solids, when the child often encounters their first real tool: the spoon. But at just six months old, the child doesn't use the spoon as a "tool" at first, as noted by how the child picks it up. At first, the child will pick up the spoon by its *head*, not its *handle*. While this approach makes sense because the head is where the food is, it isn't much different than using their fingers (and it's just as messy!).

Relevant Developments for the Hygiene Transfer (0-18 Mo)

	birth	1 *mo*	2 *mo*	3 *mo*	4 *mo*	6 *mo*	7 *mo*
Gross Motor *(Myelination)*		Holds Head (neck)			Rolls (shoulders)	Sits (torso)	
Fine Motor		Reflexive grasping			Voluntary grasping	Whole hand grasp	
Receptive Language				Turns head towards sounds		Begins to understand/responds	
Expressive Language				Smiles & coos		Babbling (canonical) *"the new cry"*	
Other Milestones		Eyesight range of 7"–30"		Tracks objects	Depth/color maturation		
Sensitive Periods		Bonding & attachment* (see more in "The Gardener," p. 103)					

 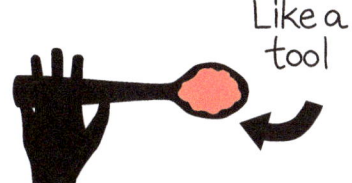

After some practice with the spoon, however, the child's hand makes the exciting shift toward reaching for the spoon by its handle (where the food isn't). This is an important milestone because it shows that the child is doing one thing (picking up the spoon) in order to accomplish another (eating food). It is here that the child begins to use objects to aid them in their pursuits—they have discovered *tools*.

So how does this relate to the hygiene tasks and when this transfer might start? Well, remember that movement is learning, right? Well, learning what tools are does not come from the awareness of knowing what the tool is. If this were the case, we would wait until *after* the child was more cognitively aware to introduce these tools (a common prescription for the utensils and the toilet). Instead, learning what tools are stems directly from the child's purposeful exploration with the tool. All hygiene tools (brushes, utensils, washcloths, and yes, even the toilet!) can be introduced at the time of sitting (at around 6 months) so that by the time the child discovers what each of these tools are for (at around 7–9 months), they are well-equipped to start using them successfully. This is the ground on which the capable toddler can stand, but only if we let them (capacity). Take a look at how these developments intersect between 6–12 months with the advent of tools in mind.

8 mo	9 mo	10 mo	11 mo	12 mo	14 mo	16 mo	18 mo
Crawls (upper legs)			Stands/cruises (lower legs)		Walks (feet)		
Thumb/fingers opposition			Pincer grasp/claps		Hand as a tool of the mind		
Knows name			Surge in understanding/ responds to simple request		Understands up to 50 words (& overextension)		
			Babbling (variegated)/points		First word (& overextension)		
		Object permanence & separation anxiety *(Can I meet my needs?)*					
					Order (1–3 years)		

setting the space for the hygiene transfer

There are a few things to note about how the child's developments intersect that will inform how we set up our spaces for these hygiene tasks. The first is that the child under six months is not able to functionally take care of themselves which is why bonding with an adult who can do these tasks for them is so important! The second is the significant motor milestones of sitting and walking. Sitting sets in motion the tool discovery timeline, and also signifies muscle control in the torso region (significant for toileting). And, walking allows the child to put a complete hygiene sequence together (i.e. *"I need to brush my teeth; I walk to the sink, climb up a stool, reach my toothbrush, and brush them"*).

What's more, however, is that language is also developing during this period. The significant shifts toward understanding after six months are not specific to just words, but includes concepts, norms, and expectations. One of the concepts the child is trying to understand is *who* is responsible for taking care of *their* body. If the young child learns in infancy that *they* are responsible for their body, its care and its actions, they will walk into toddlerhood with more capacity and a strong foundation for peer social relationships later. We can realize this potential by preparing the child's spaces so that they can meet their needs themselves. And one of the best items to have is a dresser that fits *them*.

The Child-Size Dresser

Self-dressing is a foundational skill needed in several of the hygiene tasks (namely, toileting and bathing). However, the child's clothes are often housed in adult-size dressers. The sheer lack of access to the very clothes they are trying to put on creates an unnecessary obstacle in learning this skill. In anticipation of their participation, the child-size dresser can be present from birth and once crawling, the child can start to use it! Dressers are most functional for the child when the drawers are light and have a single knob.

tools that fit & work

The idea of tools actually fitting the child's body and hands should sound rather familiar. The functionality of the tool, however, is not exactly in the tool itself, but in how we guide the child to use it. Every tool should be connected to a clear purpose (spoons are for eating, the toilet is for eliminating, etc.). If there is no purpose (we simply let the child play with it), the child will not discover what the tool is for. Explorations that appear connected to the task should be supported and those that are unproductive or unsafe should be redirected *(See Limits, pp. 38–39)*.

accessibility

While it's great to have functional, child-size tools for the child to use, those tools might as well not exist if the child cannot reach them. This makes accessibility key to the hygiene transfer. Consider the kinds of hygiene tasks you do for your child and what it might look like for them to do these themselves. This might mean adding a step stool to reach counter-height for toothbrushing; or putting plates and utensils in a low cupboard for the child to reach; or a low toilet that is not locked behind a closed bathroom door. The point is, they can't use what they can't access.

"i do it for you" (birth to 6 months)

The opportunity for the child to advocate for themselves in the first six months of life, alongside a receptive adult who is meeting their needs, allows them to enter into their *next* six months ready to start meeting their needs themselves. In the first six months, the adult feeds the child, bathes the child, changes their diapers, and just about everything else because the child cannot do these tasks for themselves just yet. And despite this, the child is still actively participating in them through communication. If their communication attempts are not stifled (with a wake-time pacifier or adult-imposed schedules in the first three months), the child is in the driver's seat in meeting their own needs. *This* is what builds the child's understanding that these needs are *theirs* and it is what gives them an avenue to advocate for their needs. This is the essence of the root of identity.

In the first six months, therefore, it is important to remember that this is *their* body, even though you are charged with taking care of it. This means that the child can make choices about their body, gain a better understanding of their body, and have an adult ready to take a step back as soon as they can do something for themselves. Let's take a look at the highlights for this from previous chapters:

movement

A low, horizontal mirror is a great aid to the child in the first six months to develop a sense of what their body is, how it moves and what it looks like. For this reason, a real mirror that gives a non-distorted image is ideal.

language

There is a rich language opportunity during the hygiene tasks to feel the parts of their body that are being named. In addition, these hygiene moments offer a template for how they will one day care for themselves.

eating

Meals are a great time for the child to advocate for their needs as they can initiate and pace the meal. By letting the child decide when they are hungry or full, they learn to listen to themselves to meet their needs.

bathing

Baby bathing[78] typically starts after the umbilical cord stump falls off (roughly 1-2 weeks after birth). Pay special attention to washing the neck, hands, and feet and remember to give the child the language of their body as you wash them. In the first few months, the child is not able to regulate their own temperature and can get cold rather quickly after a bath. Get set up ahead of time by laying out what the baby needs. Try having a front-opening onesie laid down first, then the diaper on top, and then the towel. Then, lay the baby down to dry off, remove the towel, and then, layer up!

diapering & toileting

The first step in toileting is "the feeling": the ability to correctly identify needing to "go." Newborns are especially clear about when they need a change, so what happens for the 8-month-old who will sit in poop and not say anything? Disposable diapers are often designed to make the child feel dry even though they are wet. This disconnects the child from "the feeling," which can make toileting challenging later. Consider using cloth diapers or least-absorbent[79] disposables to retain the correct information about the child's body *("When you pee, you feel wet")*.

"we do it together" (6-12 months)

This time marks the beginning of the transfer as the newly sitting child can more accurately use their hands. This ability invites the use of many hygiene tools: a toothbrush, a face cloth, a sponge, utensils, etc. While the adult will still finish each task to ensure it is done *well*, the point is to give the child the opportunity to participate now that they are able to. For most of the hygiene tasks, the child can start to participate right after sitting as there is just *one* tool and *one* requisite skill (sitting) for them to be successful. The one hygiene task that is a little more complicated, however, is toileting because the child needs several skills (and several tools) to work in unison for the child to be fully independent. For this reason, toileting is going to be our main focus as we consider the important opportunities for the hygiene transfer that appear between sitting and walking.

A Child-Size Toilet

Let's consider the steps the child needs to follow in order to toilet independently. First, the child needs to identify the sensation of needing to go, which may be felt from birth ("the feeling"). Then, the child needs to be able to hold it, which is present when the child has muscle control through the torso, i.e. sitting ("muscle control"). Next, the child needs to go to a place designated for toileting, which is established wherever the child-size toilet is placed, ideally in a *single place* at home ("location"). Finally, the child needs to get their clothing out of the way before they release, which typically becomes developmentally possible at walking ("self-dressing"). The idea, then, is to support the development of each individual skill in infancy so that by the time the child reaches toddlerhood, they can put their skills together to independently use the toilet. This approach, therefore, is not the same as "toilet training."

Toilet Orientation

The key difference between toilet *training* and toilet *orientation* is that with toilet orientation, there isn't an expectation that the child successfully uses the toilet (i.e. it doesn't matter if anything comes out). The expectation is that the child has the *opportunity* to release in somewhere aside from their diaper while they are practicing muscle control in the bladder/sphincter region (i.e. sitting). This means introducing a low infant-size toilet ("potty chair") once the child is sitting well.

How to Introduce the Toilet

It is ideal to introduce the low toilet once the child is sitting well (and not yet crawling) as the crawling child will lean out of a sitting position almost every time they sit (and won't stay on the toilet long enough to realize what it's for). But whether sitting or crawling, simply add the toilet to the diapering routine (no matter if they are wet or dry). By making this activity a predictable part of their day, they are more inclined to take advantage of the opportunity. So, at every diaper change, remove the diaper, clean them up as necessary and have them sit on the toilet. Then, let them get up *when they want* and warmly verbalize what happened (*"You peed!"* or *"Nothing came out!"*). That's it, *seriously*.

No Praise on the Potty!

Saying "great job!" may feel intuitive and supportive, but it's actually rather unproductive. Remember that the child needs no instructions to develop, they just move their body until they do? Well, they also do not need someone's opinion on how that's going. Praise[80] functions as an "external motivator" for someone who is already highly motivated to build these skills. At best, praise encourages the child to look *outward* for the reward of praise instead of looking *inward* to learn about their body. At worst, praise puts undue pressure on the child to be successful, which can make the child tense and resistant to the whole process. A friendly, warm acknowledgement of what happened is all that is needed.

The Standing Diaper Change

After sitting, the next motor milestone before walking is pulling to stand. This is relevant because the child tends to *hate* being laid *down* as soon as they can stand *up*. This passive position around body care can feel quite disempowering, especially for a child who has started to meet many of their needs themselves. Instead of continuing the struggle, try moving diaper changes upright! This standing diaper change works best when the child is positioned in front of a vertical mirror and the adult's knee holds the diaper from the back. The mirror allows the child to watch the process and see how clothes go on and off their body, essential for what's next: self-dressing.

"you do it yourself" (12 to 18 months)

This time is when the walking child has more functional use of their tools and can complete the full sequence of steps needed for each task. To empower the child to do these tasks themselves, it is helpful to first determine the steps needed to accomplish each one and then to prepare materials that will allow the child to do the task independently. For example, think of the steps needed to leave the home: the child needs to put on their shoes and coat. Consider getting shoes the child can put on by themselves and put a coat hook low enough for the child to reach. This way, the child is empowered to put their skills together to meet their needs.

Self-Dressing

Over the past six months, the child who has oriented to the toilet has begun to sort out "the feeling," "muscle control," and "the location." The last part of the toileting puzzle is "self-dressing." The child can begin some work toward self-dressing during 6–12 months of age (by orienting to where their clothes are and picking them out themselves), but most of this will require the skills of a walking child. A great way to practice this is to switch to underwear at home (once walking well). With underwear, the child gets feedback that they wouldn't get if they had stayed in a diaper (i.e. when you pee in your pants, your pants are wet). This inconvenience (as felt by both the child and the parent) is not only an incentive to put their skills to use, but it also gives the child a tremendous amount of practice with self-dressing. This works best when the child changes themselves (with some, but minimal help).

The Transition to Underwear

With the foundation of toilet orientation, the child can end up quite skilled at each individual part by the time they are 18 months old. The final push is to give them the *opportunity* to put all of the parts together by switching to underwear full time (often excluding sleep times). Do note that this is not switching to pull-ups, as pull-ups prevent the child from needing to change (which misses the point!). The transition to underwear may feel like a bit of a leap (for the child and the parent), so to make it work, the child needs time to practice, not pressure to figure it out. Your goal, therefore, is not to get the child to the toilet "on time." Instead, your goal is to prepare the environment so that they can get there themselves.

changing space

A great way to show the early toddler the exciting opportunities on the horizon is to switch out the "changing table" for a "changing space." The space can be simple and is often placed next to the child-size dresser. This space may include a mat to change on, a vertical mirror to see progress, and a small bin for them to put soiled clothes.

clothing style

Some clothes[81] make self-dressing far more complicated than it needs to be. Aim to avoid tight pants, closures (buttons, zips, or snaps), belts, and onesies at this age so that, the child will have an easier time changing themselves. The addition of a child-size dresser also helps facilitate participation in the full sequence of steps in clothing use.

the "big" toilet

Sometimes the child will want to use an adult tool, instead of the one that is built for their size (they want to be just like you!). This is especially true for the toilet. They may want to use a larger toilet (with an insert) and refuse a smaller one. Once the child is toileting more independently, they will typically switch back to the one that best fits them.

what limits capacity with hygiene tasks

The number one limiter to capacity with hygiene tasks is supporting *success* instead of *independence*. Your job is not to get good at these tasks (that's the child's job) and it can often come across as pressure instead of support when the focus is on whether the child has succeeded or not. So instead of helping them succeed, your job is to prepare their space in such a way that allows the child to be as independent as they are trying to be. And, because of the very personal nature of each hygiene task, this is an especially important mindset to have straightened out when supporting the child in this transfer. Our feelings about these hygiene tasks often get mixed up with the child's feelings about themselves, so we should tread lightly in order to support these delicate and personal moments. With that mindset in mind, let's take a look at some common hygiene limiters.

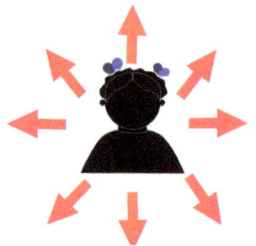

lack of opportunity

What toddlers need more than anything is more time (time we typically don't have as readily as they need it). The best way to give them more time is not in the moment, but with a 1-year head start. By introducing their tools as early as 6 months, you are just giving them more time.

lack of "the feeling"

Disposable diapers that boast "12 hours protection" are often taking *away* the feeling we want them to feel! Cloth diapers, on the other hand, protect this feeling, but do need to be changed frequently so that the child does not become accustomed to feeling wet.

a non-neutral adult

Remember, whether it be happy or sad, inserting the adult's feelings about the child and their body distracts the child from paying attention to what their body is saying or doing. This can often feel like pressure for the child to "get it right," which can cause the child to tense up.

hygiene & the budding toddler

Toilet learning is not something the child has success with one day and therefore has it sorted out for all time. Rather, it is more like the game of "Shoots and Ladders," where the child may make tremendous strides one day, and then will slide back as if they were starting from scratch the next. And while the child with the foundational skills of toilet orientation will often make a successful transition by 18 months, this is not the goal. Let's see how to keep the real goal in mind . . .

Support Independence, Not Success

As the budding toddler emerges, the child who has had toilet success in their infancy may start to resist the toilet (as early as 10–11 months). This can be confusing when it appeared this was going so smoothly! It's important, however, to recognize that it is not the toilet that they are likely resisting; it's the adult. This young child is asking to take ownership of this process (which means the adult has to take a step *back*). They become capable only if we let them be (capacity).

Wet Clothes Are Not Your Failure . . .

. . . and dry clothes are not your success! It's easy to be impressed with your own parenting skills when you have an 8-month-old infant who regularly uses the toilet. It's just as easy to be disappointed in yourself when you make the transition to underwear and there are 10 pairs of wet clothes on the first day. But this isn't your body! If you act like it's your success (are overly ecstatic) or your failure (are disappointed or frustrated), the child will place undue importance on pleasing *you*, instead of focusing on the simple fact that their clothes are wet or dry.

What You Say Matters

Wet clothes are exactly that: wet clothes. We often refer to them, however, as "accidents." This word is often associated with something negative, unwelcome, or bad (like car "accidents" or bumping someone by "accident"). This association makes it feel as though the child wetting themselves is bad (when it's just wet). So instead of, *"Did you have an accident?"* try saying, *"Are your clothes wet?"*

hygiene summary

support

keep it personal (it's about them)
support independence, not success
give opportunities, not instructions

prepare

a child-size dresser
cloth or least-absorbent diapers
child-size, functional tools

inspire

take care of them (0–6 months)
let them participate (6–12 months)
trust that they can (12–18 months)

avoid

continuing to do for the child what they can do for themselves
praise (especially with the toilet)

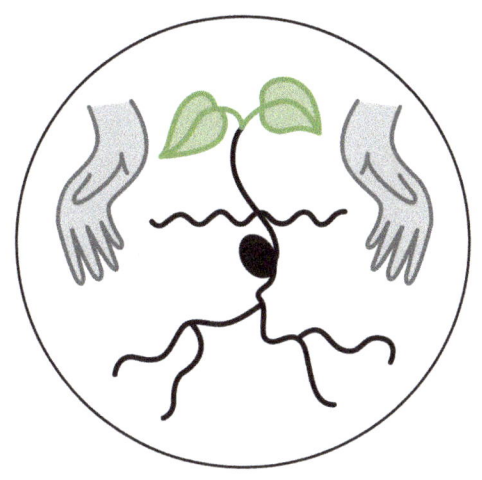

the gardener:

the adult's essential role

illustrations by:

sophia marie pappas

introduction

Welcome to the gardener! Throughout the course of this book, I have offered some ideas about your unique role in providing the essential conditions for the child to grow their roots. This section is going to focus on a cornerstone of being this gardener: bonding and attachment.

You might wonder, *"Why didn't bonding and attachment make their way into the development or conditions sections (as they are most certainly both)?"* or *"These are so important, shouldn't they be covered in the first chapter?"* Well, for starters, bonding and attachment are not things the child does on their own from the start (like the "roots") and they aren't things that get transferred at some point (like the "conditions"). They're kind of a two-person gig the whole time. But let me explain why I have left them until the end.

You have just read the unfolding story of the child from birth to 18 months of age and hopefully have built an understanding of what the child is trying to do developmentally and how you can help them. What's left to cover is how we are with them, the relationship we have, and the bond we create. But this relationship, while immensely important, does evoke some very real and very personal feelings from us. Sometimes our thoughts and feelings about bonding and attachment can overshadow the child and their important developments. For instance, it may be hard to set limits around screen time if the child is kicking and screaming for it and we just want to have a "pleasant evening with them." Unfortunately, this inadvertently shows the child that kicking and screaming works, so they should keep communicating in those ways. It may also be difficult to appreciate the child's growing capacity if our focus is only on their separation from *us* and not on the exciting attachments they're making. Any one of these can turn into challenging learning dispositions both at home and at school, which will negatively impact bonding and attachment with us and the other adults in their lives in the future. So, while we want our love and affection for our child to be real and tangible, it shouldn't be at the cost of their other pursuits.

Think of the child's developmental "inputs" (movement, language, food, bonding, etc.) like the different members of a band. Bonding isn't the lead singer; it's the bass—reliable, palpable in the background to everything else that's going on. You almost forget that it's there until you can't hear it, and you realize how much it was adding. It's what we stand on, not what we're reaching for. So, while we give that unconditional love to our child, we should do so within the context of *their* development (which is why this chapter comes last). Let's now take a look at why bonding exists in the first place.

Why Bonding Matters

At their core, bonding and attachment are survival mechanisms[82] to make up for the fact that humans are born considerably underdeveloped. By bonding with *someone* who will help them meet their needs, the young newborn is given the necessary time to develop the capacity to meet their needs themselves. But this "bond" is more than just a *feeling* that the young infant's needs are being met; it's this overall sense of security that their needs *will be* met. This significant difference is what led Montessori to call the initial months of bonding the child's "first basic trust."[83] This is a trust the child develops in their environment to meet their basic needs and it is largely built in the first few months. To appreciate how important this trust is in the child's life, let's imagine the child on their first day of school, a

new job or a big life transition of relocation, a loss or other adjustment. Someone with this basic trust is someone who, despite being lost or uncertain, will go find people who can help them. When a child does not have responsive adults in the months after birth, the child may struggle to build this agency,[84] this trust. They are not sure if they can survive, aren't sure who to ask for help, and may not believe—at their core—that those people exist. It has the potential to be the lens through which the child sees the world.[85] So let's take a look at how we can prepare the space for the development of the essential skills of bonding and attachment and then look more closely at this important early time.

setting the space for bonding

Bonding and attachment are built through the day in, day out responsiveness of the adults to meet the child's needs. Your work to bond with your child is never really over, of course, it's just that the early months are especially significant to this young child in establishing this bond. It is important to highlight that this responsiveness is not built in one day (nor is it destroyed in one day). So give yourself a break if you don't feel that immediate connection. This bond *grows* over time. The focus is not on how much you love them on day one, but rather on being responsive to their needs. That sounds pretty simple, right? Well . . .

Imagine that I asked you to tie your shoe (seems simple), but you had to do it while you were riding a roller coaster (not so simple).

While responsiveness is the essential element in the formation of this basic trust, we have to remember *when* the bulk of this trust is being formed: in the first few months after birth. This is a time when parents have to be the most on (to meet the 24/7 needs of the baby) and when they may be feeling the most off (physically, emotionally, and mentally). And anytime something is *difficult* for the parent and *critical* for the child, this becomes a *red flag* for support. The best path forward for the child, therefore, is actually beyond just being responsive; it's about preparing an environment of support for the adult so that they actually can respond as they intend to do.* And my postpartum recipe for this is what I call . . .

---

* The PEACE Program was started in 2016 in response to this idea. We offer free support groups, personalized home visits, and parenting workshops. Learn more at www.thepeaceprogram.org.

Responsiveness

We know that meeting the child's needs is important, but we often don't know exactly what they are at first (sometimes we think they are hungry when they're actually tired). Bonding is about *responding* to the child, not getting it right every time. Some response times are faster, and others are slower. Keep trying! In time, you will learn what your child is saying and more accurately meet their needs.

Environment

The child's growth is highly dependent on the kinds of experiences they have; their environment matters! By preparing the space for *you* to be successful, you will have carved out the time to better respond to your child. This might mean gathering the supplies you need (water, snacks, etc.) before you settle into a feeding or setting up the child's play space well before they need it so that it is ready as soon as a new development arises.

Support

Because of the many needs newborns have, it can help if the adults caring for the child have someone to help care for them, as well. Say "yes" to help and get the support you need to reduce stress and loneliness. Your child does not need a martyr; they need *you*. There are parents feeling the same way as you right now—make every effort to find them. Show visitors this page as a reminder to help with meals, laundry, dishes, etc. Whatever helps you right now, helps the child.

Touch

Touch (especially skin-to-skin) releases the "bonding" hormone oxytocin[86] for both the child and the adult (so it makes everyone feel good and connected). Additionally, touch aids bonding because it reassures the child that they don't have to go very far to get help. The impact of touch in bonding is especially true when connecting with the birthing mother. This physical reconnection (immediately after birth, if possible) gives the child the opportunity to reconnect with someone familiar, which can expedite the formation of this trust.

bonding & the first 6 weeks

I hope it is clear at this point that in order to provide the kind of responsiveness the child needs to establish this basic trust, the adults caring for the infant need our support. This is especially true during the 6–8-week period after birth on account of the many challenges, especially for the birthing mother.[87] There's the lack of sleep, physical injuries, and the pendulum of hormones taking the birthing mother from very high highs . . . to very low lows. But the one challenge that I think takes the cake for any parent (birthing or not) is the surprising depth of lonely insecurity that you aren't doing whatever this is supposed to look like "right."

There's this persistent question (or doubt) of *"Can I really do this?"* that can mark this time. And while this question is troubling to us as parents, it can actually be an important lifeline to bonding with our child. You see, *your* question is actually the same as the *child's* question.

The child wants to know if their environment (you) can meet their needs, just as you are wondering if you will be able to. The child, therefore, is not the only one building this basic trust; you are building a basic trust in yourself, as well. I have come to see that these two trusts are formed at the same time through the simple act of responding to the child. Every time you respond, the child learns that they really can trust this environment to meet their needs; and you learn that you really can do this (because you already are). While Dr. Montessori didn't outline a "parent's basic trust," she did describe a level of connectedness between the adult and child in the 6–8 weeks after birth that she called the "Symbiotic Period."[88]

the symbiotic period

Dr. Montessori observed a quite literal "symbiosis" between a birthing mother and a breastfeeding child in the 6-8 weeks after birth that became a template for how she translated these important first few months of bonding. Through breastfeeding, she observed, the child received this important nourishment, and with that action, the mother's uterus was aided in shrinking back to normal size. One action met the needs of both people. This idea of a symbiotic relationship can aid the adults caring for the newborn to maximize bonding through these deeply personal feeding moments with the young child. If breastfeeding, this is a time of quite literal re-attachment after the separation of birth. If bottle-feeding, this can be a time to lean into skin-to-skin feeding to support this bonding opportunity. And while Dr. Montessori's ideas around the symbiotic period centered around the 6–8 weeks after birth, I found this idea of symbiosis to be so profound that I began to see it as a "mirrored experience" that extended far beyond these early months.

Mirrored Experiences

When the child experiences something, the adult in relationship with that child experiences the same thing in their own way, and vice versa (i.e. if labor was long for you, it was equally long for the child; if you are tired because you were up with the child all night, the child is also tired for the exact same reason). This idea of "mirrored experiences," however, is not just for the sake of having a healthy dose of empathy (though that is always helpful). This idea offers an important window into the child's development. You see, by seeing you and your child's experiences as a mirror of one another's, you can better understand their development by simply examining your own feelings about it. So, if things just got really hard for you, it's likely because something big just developed in your child. Moreover, because the child's developmental shifts are relatively predictable, we can actually take this a step further to predict the times that will likely be hardest for the adult. The developmental timelines, therefore, are a roadmap for when *you* might need more support. Remember that bonding is much easier when the adult is well supported so that they have the bandwidth to respond to the child. Knowing when the rough patches will be allows you to preemptively carve out that support. Let's build this roadmap by starting with some "big picture" ideas about the child's development.

the four "planes" of development

Humans develop in distinct stages (or "planes," as Dr. Montessori called them), from birth to about age 24 (when the person is basically "mature," developmentally speaking). This "birth to maturity" period can be broken down into the following four planes[89]: infancy (birth to 6 years), childhood (6–12 years), adolescence (12–18 years), and maturity (18–24 years). The big transition point within this 24-year span is, of course, puberty. Puberty marks the transition from the development of the child (birth to 12 years) to the development of the adult (12–24 years). And while this should all sound pretty familiar from our own lives, Dr. Montessori articulated something essential to understanding how development unfolds over time: an **identical** pattern in each 12-year block.[90]

Infancy		Childhood	Adolescence		Maturity
0–3 yr	3–6 yr	6–12 yr	12–15 yr	15–18 yr	18–24 yr
Development of the Child			*Development of the Adult*		
Development	Refinement	Growth	Development	Refinement	Growth

Each 12-year segment starts with a period of rapid development (birth to 3 years and 12–15 years). These periods of rapid development are then followed by a period of what Dr. Montessori described as "refinement," which is basically to say that the child isn't developing new things insomuch as they are adjusting and refining whatever they just developed. For example, the child is rapidly developing the ability to walk and talk in the first three years, but then switches to regulating those actions and words in the subsequent three years (3–6). This is also true for the period of adolescence because while most of the changes in puberty happen in the three years after its onset (12–15 years, generally), there are an additional three years (15–18) that are still part of puberty development, just more refined. The last part is a period of relatively stable growth: developmentally, the 6–12-year-old child basically just gets taller and swaps out their baby teeth with adult teeth. 18–24 years is also mostly steady, stable *developmental* growth.

This pattern (development, refinement, growth) is what got me thinking about this initial period of rapid development of the first three years. Would it be possible that this pattern exists on a smaller scale as well? Sure enough, it did . . .

development, refinement, growth *(repeat)*

In the first trimester of pregnancy, the embryo is building all of the organs and body systems of the will-be fetus: hands, feet, lungs, heart, etc. (rapid development). In the second trimester, the fetus is "fine-tuning" that development by putting these systems to use and further polishing off their formation (refinement). The final trimester is a time when the fetus is packing on weight in anticipation of birth (growth). The appearance of this pattern was so striking that I continued my query into the next stage of development: the "External Pregnancy."[91]

"External Pregnancy"

Dr. Montessori theorized that birth has a period of roughly nine months of dependence on either side of it (an *internal* pregnancy and a subsequent *external* pregnancy) where the adult carries the child and meets nearly all of their needs. The culmination of this "external pregnancy" was around nine months when the child crawled. Crawling represents a significant moment of exodus akin to a "second birth" when the child can move themselves and has started to meet many of their own needs (self-feeding, independent sleeping, toilet orientation, etc.). In looking at these nine months after birth as a "pregnancy" with trimesters of their own, this same pattern emerged: *development, refinement, growth*. The first three months after birth is a time of rapid development (in eyesight, the first basic trusts, circadian rhythms, etc.). The second three months of age (3–6 months) is all about "fine-tuning" what came before (eyesight refines to color and depth perception, sleep matures, the hand refines to grasping, etc). And the final three months before crawling (roughly 6–9 months) marks a period of relatively stable growth (the child sits and stays). And although the "external pregnancy" theory ends at nine months, this idea of a "second birth" seemed to me to give way to a "second postpartum" with yet another cycle of development, refinement, and growth. The three months after crawling (roughly 9–12 months) are marked by rapid development: teething, the second basic trust, crawling, cruising, etc. 12–15 months is typically all about refinement: early mobilities turn into walking and early language skills to talking. Finally, the 15–18-month-old infant returns to steady growth before diving into the next period of rapid development: toddlerhood (18–36 months). I've compiled this theory into what I call "The Gardener's Chart."

the gardener's chart

	Pregnancy			0–9 Months ("External Pregnancy")		
	0–3 mo	3–6 mo	6–9 mo	0–3 mo	3–6 mo	6–9 mo
	Conception			**Birth**		
	Development	Refinement	Growth	Development	Refinement	Growth
	Developing the body	Fine-tuning the body	Growing the body	Developing basic trust in environment to meet needs	Fine-tuning in sleep, senses, digestion, movement	Using capacity: self-feeding, independent sleeping, toilet orientation
Level of Difficulty for Parent & Child				HARD	EASIER	EASIEST
Basic Approach to Parent & Child				SUPPORT	ACT	TRUST

The First Trimesters

The first trimesters are times that the child is developing rapidly. This means that there is a lot of adjustment on the part of the adult (lots of personal growth for the parent during these times!). This makes these times *hard*. Remember that everyone is working hard during these times (especially the child). Support, therefore, is the essential element during these first trimesters. Plan for it, ask for it, accept it, and give it, liberally. You can use these "red times" to recognize why you might feel frayed and actively advocate for more support.

The Second Trimesters

The second trimesters are times that the child is fine-tuning their recent developments. This means that there is a lot of *opportunity* to use the environment to maximize the child's recent achievements. These tend to be times where the adult is less challenged relative to the previous trimester, but still not "out of the woods." Actively preparing an environment to take advantage of these times is the essential element during these second trimesters. This means giving opportunities for and removing obstacles to the child's independence.

	9–18 Months			18–36 Months	3–6 Years	6–12 Years
	9–12 mo	12–15 mo	15–18 mo	18–36 mo	3–6 yr	6–12 yr
	Mobility			**"Me!"**		
	Development	Refinement	Growth	Development	Refinement	Growth
	Developing basic trust in self to meet needs, separation anxiety, teeth, motor skills	Fine-tuning movement (walking), language (talking), underwear orientation	Using capacity: self-directed movements, language, toilet independence	Developing responsibility of self & capacity for self-care	Fine-tuning movement & language with self-regulation & literacy	Using previously built capacities to think for oneself
	HARD	EASIER	EASIEST	HARD	EASIER	EASIEST
	SUPPORT	ACT	TRUST	SUPPORT	ACT	TRUST

The Third Trimesters

The third trimesters are times when the child is using all of the abilities they've built over the past two trimesters. This means that there is a "letting go" on part of the adult to allow the child to take ownership of whatever they worked so hard to develop. Trust, therefore, is the essential element during these third trimesters; a trust in the child *and* a trust in yourself. The third trimesters tend to be the easiest times for the adult, with one important clarification: the next cycle of maturity does not begin with the listed age (read that again). Rather, the next cycle begins with one of the four events[92] that initiate a period of rapid development: *conception*, *birth*, *mobility* and *"me."* This is important to note because these aren't always so perfectly timed. The third trimesters, unfortunately, are often at risk of being cut short with an early-arriving period of rapid development. This can deeply impact the experience for the adult. If, for example, a child is born premature or starts crawling at six months of age (instead of nine), the child and the adult have a little less time to breathe between big developmental strides. Moreover, these early-arriving first trimesters may only elongate the period, rather than bump up the timeline. In these cases, the essential elements are both support and trust.

using the gardener's chart

The intended use of The Gardener's Chart is to provide a template for you to make your own chart, based on your child's development. By tailoring these ideas to the child in front of you, you will be able to recognize the times when you need the most support, take advantage of the learning opportunities

SOLINA — SUPPORT — ACT — TRUST
4 DAY (100 HOUR) LABOR
BIRTH — 3 — 6

After 4 days of labor, I was exhausted. I struggled during this whole period. Solina hated the swaddle and loved being rocked and held.

I felt much better during 3–6 months, and there was so much learning for Solina: sleeping, rolling, and grasping. She loved motion and finally could rock and roll herself to sleep independently.

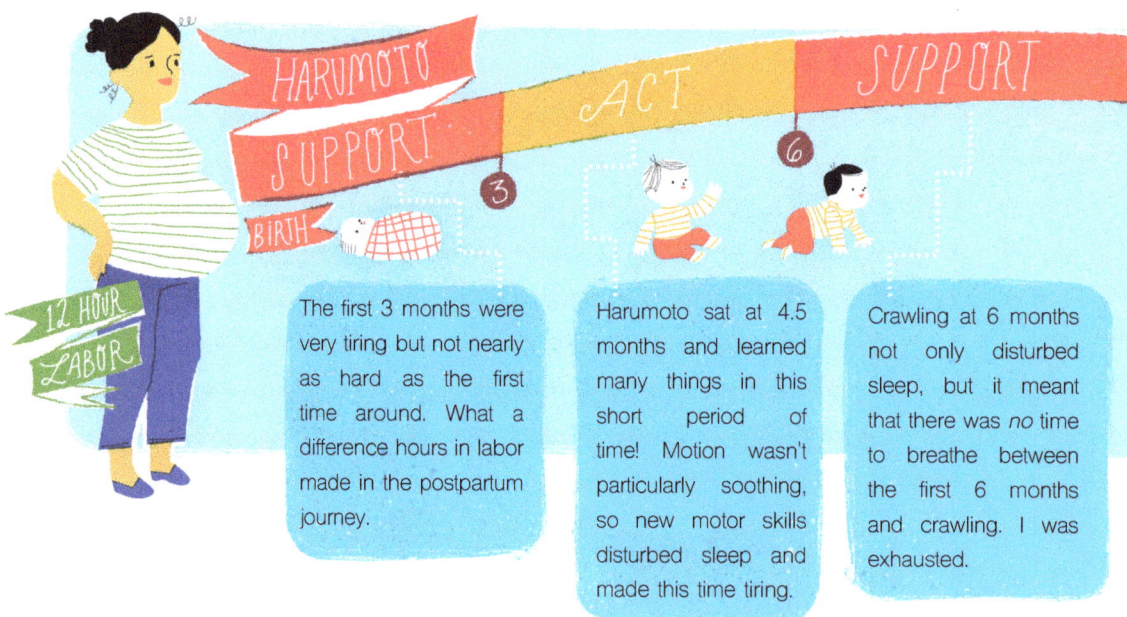

HARUMOTO — SUPPORT — ACT — SUPPORT
12 HOUR LABOR
BIRTH — 3 — 6

The first 3 months were very tiring but not nearly as hard as the first time around. What a difference hours in labor made in the postpartum journey.

Harumoto sat at 4.5 months and learned many things in this short period of time! Motion wasn't particularly soothing, so new motor skills disturbed sleep and made this time tiring.

Crawling at 6 months not only disturbed sleep, but it meant that there was *no* time to breathe between the first 6 months and crawling. I was exhausted.

during refinement, and take a step back during times when your child is ready to soar. To illustrate this, let's take a look at two examples of my two children's developmental timelines and what their Gardener's Charts told me about support, opportunity, and trust.

What a gift these months were of sitting and not yet crawling! From her independent playtime to self-feeding to using the toilet, 6–9 months was such a time of growth. I felt like I could finally catch my breath.

Solina had intense separation anxiety once crawling, which lasted for *months*. Along with frequent teething, this made the 9–12 month time very difficult and tiring.

Separation anxiety finally faded almost as soon as Solina started walking. She also had new words, started underwear, and even self-weaned during these 12–15 months.

15–18 months felt like a well-deserved pause before toddlerhood! Solina said "Me!" at 17 months, and we felt ready for what was next.

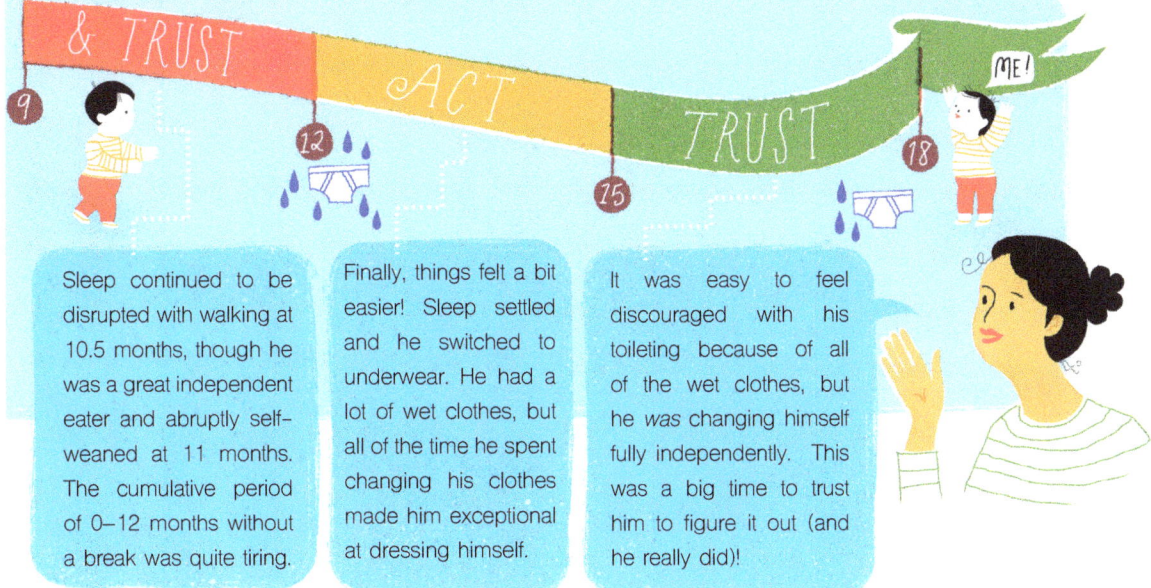

Sleep continued to be disrupted with walking at 10.5 months, though he was a great independent eater and abruptly self-weaned at 11 months. The cumulative period of 0–12 months without a break was quite tiring.

Finally, things felt a bit easier! Sleep settled and he switched to underwear. He had a lot of wet clothes, but all of the time he spent changing his clothes made him exceptional at dressing himself.

It was easy to feel discouraged with his toileting because of all of the wet clothes, but he *was* changing himself fully independently. This was a big time to trust him to figure it out (and he really did)!

gardener summary

support

be present

respond

keep talking

prepare

get set up ahead of time

plan for support

predict the hard times

inspire

respond & touch (0–6 months)

aid independence (6–12 months)

grow with them (12–18 months)

avoid

wake-time pacifier

adult-imposed schedules

getting down on yourself

the full chart:

putting it together: birth to 18 months

illustrations by:

alisha nicole brumfield tracy nishimura bishop brenda brambila

"The child is not an inert being who owes everything he can do to us, as if he were an empty vessel that we have to fill. No, it is the child who makes the man, and no man exists who was not made by the child he once was."

— Maria Montessori, *The Absorbent Mind*[93]

full chart illustrations by:

alisha nicole brumfield *(0-6 mo)*   tracy nishimura bishop *(6-12 mo)*   brenda brambila *(12-18 mo)*

conclusion

Welcome to the full charts—you made it! You are now ready to put these ideas together in a roadmap of support for not only your child, but for yourself during these first essential 18 months of your child's life. And if you're arriving here because you've skipped ahead, *go back*. Trust me on this, start from the beginning, and I'll look forward to seeing you here after you do. And now that we're here, I want to leave you with a few final thoughts before sending you off on your parenting journey. Infancy is all about trusting the process. You will not see the fruits of your labor—or theirs—until *at least* toddlerhood (and probably much later than that!). Keep your child's development at the center of your questions, and rely on your own observations to make adjustments as your child grows. You will get things wrong. *And* you will get things right. It's hard, and you will get through it. My hope is that you find community along the way, and find ways to give your child the time and space to grow as they were born to do.

The Full Charts

In the following timelines, you will see some familiar ideas represented and outlined. First, you will see a banner along the top of each chart depicting the cycles of maturity from The Gardener's Chart.

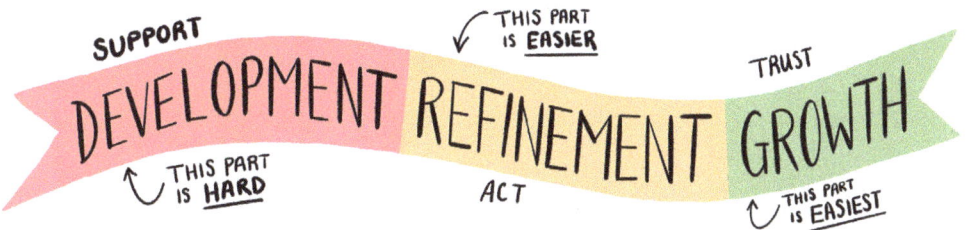

Along the bottom of the chart, you will see another banner depicting the progression of the "transfer" of the conditions from the adult to the child:

ADULT MEETS CHILD'S NEEDS | ADULT & CHILD MEET CHILD'S NEEDS | CHILD MEETS CHILD'S NEEDS

In addition, next to each illustration, a page number is listed so you can reference that page in the book for more specific ideas about that particular development or recommendation. Ready? Let's take a look at the full charts.

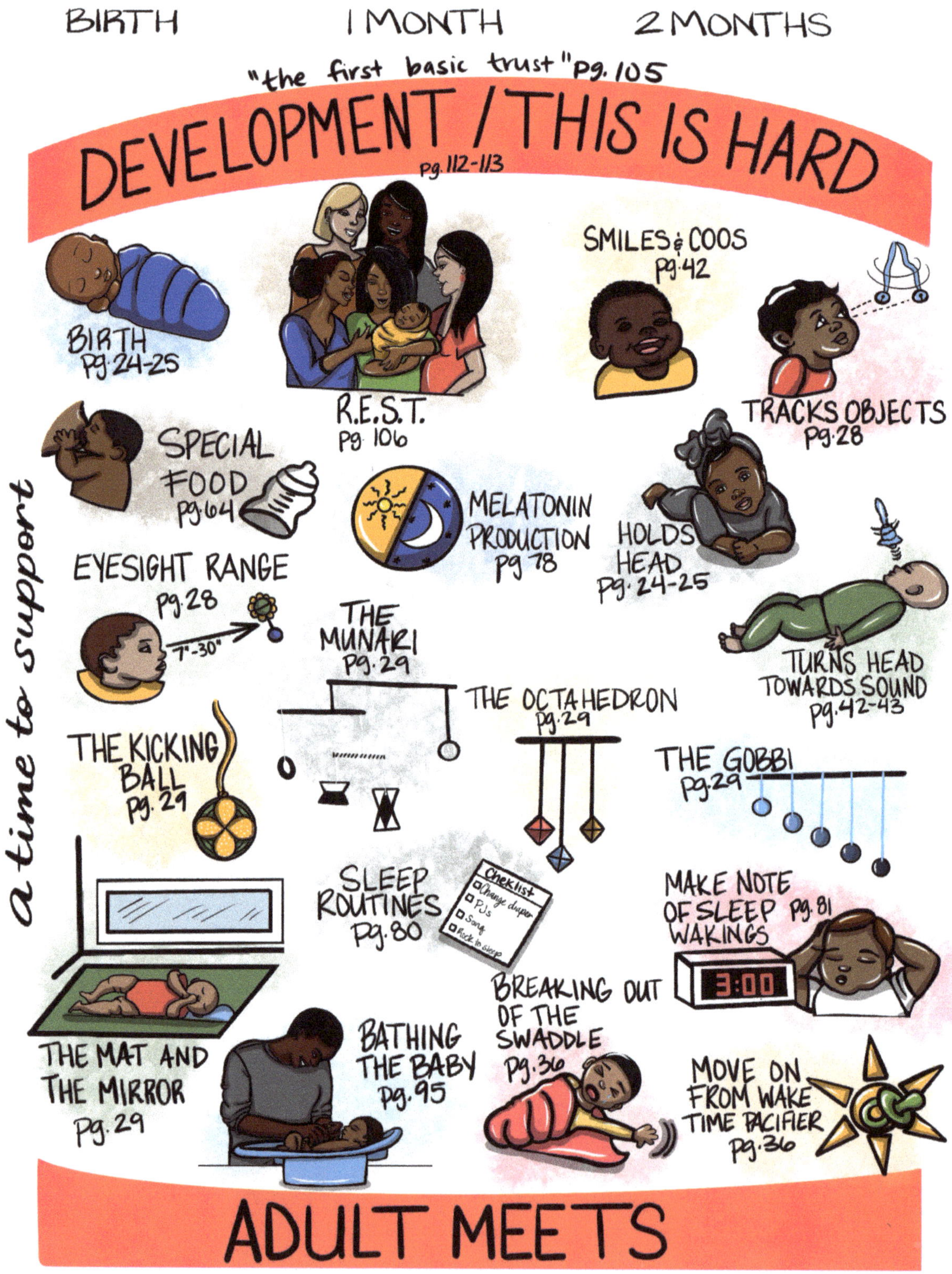

BIRTH
1 MONTH
2 MONTHS
"the first basic trust" pg. 105
DEVELOPMENT / THIS IS HARD
pg. 112-113
BIRTH Pg. 24-25
R.E.S.T. Pg. 106
SMILES & COOS Pg. 42
TRACKS OBJECTS Pg. 28
SPECIAL FOOD Pg. 64
MELATONIN PRODUCTION Pg 78
HOLDS HEAD Pg. 24-25
EYESIGHT RANGE Pg. 28
7"-30"
THE MUNARI Pg. 29
TURNS HEAD TOWARDS SOUND Pg. 42-43
THE OCTAHEDRON Pg. 29
THE KICKING BALL Pg. 29
THE GOBBI Pg. 29
a time to support
SLEEP ROUTINES Pg. 80
Checklist
Change diaper
PJs
Song
Rock to sleep
MAKE NOTE OF SLEEP WAKINGS Pg. 81
3:00
BREAKING OUT OF THE SWADDLE Pg. 36
THE MAT AND THE MIRROR Pg. 29
BATHING THE BABY Pg. 95
MOVE ON FROM WAKE TIME PACIFIER Pg. 36
ADULT MEETS

3 MONTHS 4 MONTHS 5 MONTHS

REFINEMENT/THIS IS EASIER
pg. 112-113

BEGINS TO GRASP pg. 24-25

ROLLS pg. 24-25

TONGUE-THRUST REFLEX FADES pg. 60

a time to act

INDEPENDENT PLAY pg. 28

DEPTH PERCEPTION & COLOR MATURATION pg. 28

HANDHELD TEETHERS pg. 29

SPOONFULS OF NATURAL FRUIT JUICES pg. 65

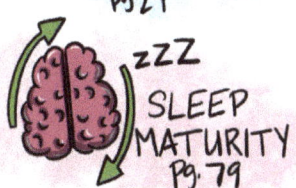
SLEEP MATURITY pg. 79

GRASPING TOYS pg. 29

CONSISTENT WHERE AND HOW OF SLEEP pg. 82

3-5 DAYTIME NAPS pg. 85

CHILD'S NEEDS

6 months   7 months   8 months

GROWTH / THIS IS EASIEST
PAGE 112 – 113

a time to trust

SITS
PAGE 24-25

CANONICAL BABBLING
PAGE 42-43

WHOLE HAND GRASP
PAGE 24-25

THUMB-FINGER OPPOSITION
PAGE 24-25

CENTRAL INSISORS
PAGE 60-61

DIGESTIVE MATURITY
PAGE 60-61

BEGINS TO UNDERSTAND/RESPONDS
PAGE 42-43

KNOWS NAME
PAGE 42-43

2-3 NAPS
PAGE 85

TOOLS FOR GROOMING
PAGE 96

SPOON & MAT
PAGE 67

LOW TOILET
PAGE 96

TEETHERS
PAGE 30

PLATE & CUP
PAGE 67

LOW OPEN SHELF
PAGE 31

ADULT + CHILD MEET

DEVELOPMENT / THIS IS HARD

9 months — **10 months** — **11 months**

the second basic trust PAGE 30
PAGE 112 – 113

a time to support

CRAWLS
PAGE 24-25

STANDS
PAGE 24-25

CRUISES
PAGE 24-25

PINCER GRASP
PAGE 24-25

CLAPS
PAGE 24-25

POINTS
PAGE 24-25

VARIEGATED BABBLING
PAGE 42-43
("BALAMADA")

SURGE IN UNDERSTANDING
PAGE 42-43
("BALL")

2 NAPS
PAGE 85

LATERAL INCISORS
PAGE 60-61

OBJECT PERMANENCE
PAGE 31

SEPARATION ANXIETY
PAGE 32

FAMILY FOOD
PAGE 67

SLEEP INTERRUPTIONS
PAGE 84

THE CHILD-SIZE DRESSER
PAGE 92

FORK & BOWL
PAGE 67

STANDING DIAPER CHANGE
PAGE 97

TOYS WITH SEQUENCE
PAGE 31

CHILD'S NEEDS

about the illustrations

Mariana Bissonnette *(she/her)* is an AMI 0–6 Montessori educator and parent of two. The illustrations in *Babies Build Toddlers* serve several functions to bring this book to life. Not only do these illustrations help visualize child development for sleep-deprived readers, but they purposefully come from more than one perspective.

Mariana was born and raised in the San Francisco Bay area and grew up in a family with strong roots to her grandmother's home country of Venezuela. This provided a home environment with multiple perspectives, languages, cultures, and approaches. With this background, and in being a white author, it was important to Mariana that the children and their development were not illustrated by just one person. *Babies Build Toddlers*, therefore, features a talented team of illustrators so that a variety of illustrative styles, backgrounds, and perspectives were visualizing this important development in infancy. Mariana's hope is that readers will look at the same development through a new lens in each chapter to validate that there is not just one way to support the child's development. Check out this amazing team:

Alisha Nicole Brumfield *(Eating, Full Chart)*

Lisha Nicole *(she/her)* is a self-taught acrylic painter and digital illustrator currently based in Houston, TX. Falling in love with art at a young age, her art has always been inspired by bold and beautiful people and their vibrancy that glows from within. Lisha has participated in art exhibitions and events and her work currently represents life, love, culture, and diversity.

Brenda Brambila *(The Plant, Hygiene, Full Chart)*

Brenda Citlali Brambila Flores *(she/her)* is a self-taught illustrator and Mexico native who was raised in Chicago while being undocumented for 15 years. Her activism and work have kept the undocumented struggle at a center. She has always had an interest in arts and illustration, but due to being undocumented, she was unable to pursue it academically until she taught herself how to create digital art.

Esma Bošnjaković *(The Plant, Language)*

Esma *(she/her)* is a self-described "free-time" illustrator, born and raised in beautiful Vienna, Austria. She started doing art as a hobby on the side only recently, and it has since changed her life in the best possible way! Esma loves creating illustrations that counter stereotypes and portray Muslim women as they really are—surprisingly ordinary.

Samantha Morales-Johnson *(Movement)*

Samantha Morales-Johnson *(she/her)* is a Southern California native and an active member of her tribe, the Gabreleno/Tongva Band of Mission Indians. Samantha is a science illustrator and strongly believes in the importance of illustrated books beyond childhood. She also enjoys teaching children (particularly swimming)!

Sophia Marie Pappas *(Acknowledgements, Introduction, The Gardener)*

Sophia *(she/her)* is a Pittsburgh-based illustrator creating work for magazines, children's publishing, and greeting cards. She has had the pleasure of working with Google's San Francisco offices, F&W Media, Attic Studio Publishing, NPR, and American Greetings. Her work is inspired by her love of printmaking and people watching.

Tracy Nishimura Bishop *(The Plant, Sleeping, Conclusion, Full Chart)*

Tracy Nishimura Bishop *(she/her)* is a San Francisco Bay area-based illustrator and has illustrated more than 20 picture and chapter books. She grew up in a U.S. Army base in Japan and discovered her love of drawing through manga and anime. She also loves collecting pens, reading, and going on walks with her very hairy dog named Harry.

Chie Ushio *(Cover & Title Page)*

Chie Ushio *(she/her)* was born and raised in Tokyo, Japan. She graduated from the School of Visual Arts, New York in 2004 and worked as a designer at Penguin Random House for 11 years. She now works as a design consultant for various clients. She loves dogs, sewing, and good sushi.

A Note about Language

Dr. Maria Montessori (1870–1952) was a fervent advocate for women's rights and equality. Despite overcoming the obstacles she faced as an aspiring female scientist and physician (among her later pursuits in education), her written language continues to reinforce patriarchal references to the child as "he" and "him," as well as using "man" and "mankind" as if they were all-encompassing terms for humanity. Moreover, these terms have historically and systematically excluded Black, Indigenous, and People of the Global Majority from this generalized "humanity" that we are meant to extrapolate from these white-male centered terms. I considered amending Dr. Montessori's quotes to "they/them" and "humankind" in an effort to not perpetuate the harm caused by them. Upon reflection, however, I decided to leave the quotes in their original form so that we may continue to notice and name the sexist and racist language in our reference books, recognize the harm caused by them, and more broadly, actively work to shift our systems and policies toward true equity by removing the artificially created obstacles that privilege some on the backs of others.

References & Further Reading

Introduction

1   In *The Absorbent Mind* (page 132), Dr. Montessori refers to "helpers in the home" for which there is a footnote about the special training courses for these "Helpers" ("Assistenti Infanzia Montessoriane") conducted by the Montessori Society of Rome.

2   **Capitalization & Race:** There is debate on whether or not to capitalize racial words. There is a further debate about which ones to capitalize, especially "white." I have chosen in this book to capitalize Black, Indigenous, and People of the Global Majority. I have chosen not to capitalize "white." As someone who presents as white, and while systemic inequality based on race persists, I feel this is one way to de-center whiteness and amplify Black, Indigenous, and People of the Global Majority.

3   **People of the Global Majority:** I first heard this term at the 2019 Montessori for Social Justice (www.montessoriforsocialjustice.org) conference in Portland, OR. This term is meant to be an alternative or counter to the term "People of Color," as that term centers whiteness (with the focus being on those who are "not-white" and therefore "of color"). People of the Global Majority is far more inclusive and intentionally uses non-marginalizing language of "majority" in the recognition that people considered "white" are the global minority, not the majority.

4   On July 13, 2013 "three radical Black organizers—Alicia Garza, Patrisse Cullors, and Opal Tometi—created a Black-centered political will and movement building project called #BlackLivesMatter. It was in response to the acquittal of Trayvon Martin's murderer, George Zimmerman" (www.blacklivesmatter.com/herstory). July 13, 2020 marked the 7th anniversary of the Black Lives Matter movement that gained international solidarity following the murders of Breonna Taylor and George Floyd at the hands of police in the Spring of 2020.

5   **Quote:** *The Absorbent Mind* (page 2) by Dr. Maria Montessori

6   **Aid to Life:** "This is education, understood as a help to life; an education from birth, which feeds a peaceful revolution and unites all in a common aim, attracting them as to a single centre." —*The Absorbent Mind* (page 16) by Maria Montessori

7   **Self-Construction:** "It is true that in all these activities, the child may be said to be playing. But this kind of play is effortful, and it leads him to acquire the new powers which will be needed for his future . . . [T]his kind of effort is proper to childhood, and that is why I say that imitativeness in children is a kind of inspiration which leads them to self-constructive work." —*The Absorbent Mind* (pages 187–8) by Maria Montessori

8   **The Growth of a Seed:** "This idea came from the observation of the seed of a plant, which contains, hidden between the two cotyledons, a tiny plant in which we can recognise root and leaves and which, set in the earth, develops into the new plant. It was supposed that an analogous process held good for animals and for man." —*The Secret of Childhood* (page 13) by Maria Montessori

9   **The Absorbent Mind:** "The comparison we have already made helps us to understand this power the child has of absorbing from his surroundings. There are some insects which look like leaves and others which look like stalks. They pass their lives on leaves and stalks, which they resemble so perfectly as to seem completely one with them. Something like this happens in the child. He absorbs the life going on about him and becomes one with it, just as these insects become one with the vegetation on which they live. The child's impressions are so profound that a biological or psycho-chemical change takes place, by which his mind ends by resembling the environment itself. Children become like the things they love. In every type of life it has been discovered that this power exists, of absorbing the environment and coming to resemble it." —*The Absorbent Mind* (page 108) by Maria Montessori

10   **Incarnation:** "This mind, which receives all, does not judge, does not refuse, does not react. It

absorbs everything and incarnates it in the coming man. The child performs this work of incarnation to achieve equality with other men, and to adapt himself to live with them." —*The Absorbent Mind* (page 304) by Maria Montessori

11	**Critical Periods/Sensitive Periods:** "One important concept in developmental research is that of "critical" or "sensitive" periods. These are times when the brain is in an active period of growth and change. At these times, skills may need a certain degree of stimulation in order to develop fully. You might think of it as a window of opportunity when skill practice or teaching will be most effective." —*Your Child's Growing Mind* (page 24) by Jane M. Healy

12	**Sensitive Periods/Hugo DeVries:** "In biology these [sensitive] periods were first studied by DeVries, and are particularly apparent in living creatures that reach their adult state through metamorphoses, as in the case of insects. We may take, for instance, the butterfly caterpillar. It must feed on very tender leaves, and yet the butterfly lays its eggs in the most hidden fork of the branch, near the trunk of the tree. Who will show the little caterpillars hidden there, the moment they leave the egg, that the tender leaves they need are to be found at the extreme tip of the branch, in the light? Now the caterpillar is strongly sensible to light; light attracts it, summons it as by an, irresistible voice, fascinates it, and the caterpillar goes wriggling towards where 'he light is brightest, till it reaches the tip of the branch, and thus finds itself, famished for food, among the budding leaves that can give it nourishment. It is a strange fact that when the caterpillar has passed through its first stage and is full grown, it can eat other food, and then it loses its sensibility to light." —*The Secret of Childhood* (page 35) by Maria Montessori

13	**Sensitive Period for Movement:** "All movement thus has a most intricate and delicate machinery. But in man none of it is established at birth. It has to be formed and perfected by the child's activity in the world. Unlike the animals, man finds himself so richly endowed with muscles that there are hardly any movements he cannot learn to make, and while he is doing this we do not talk about strengthening his muscles, but of coordinating them, which is a very different thing." —*The Absorbent Mind* (page 151) by Maria Montessori

14	**Sensitive Period for Language:** "But how is speech formed after birth? . . . [A] concentration of sensitiveness in the centres for language, especially in that which accumulates words. I reason that these centres are specially designed for the capture of language, of words; so it may be that this powerful hearing mechanism only responds and acts in relation to sounds of a particular kind—those of speech. The result is that words heard by the child set in motion the complicated mechanism by which he makes the movements needed to reproduce them. If there were no special isolation of the sensitivity which directs this—if the centres were free to welcome every kind of sound—the child would start making the most astonishing noises. He would imitate all those peculiar to the place where he happened to be, including the non-human ones. It is only because nature has constructed and isolated these centres for the purpose of language, that the child ever learns to speak at all." —*The Absorbent Mind* (page 127) by Maria Montessori

15	**Sensitive Period for Order:** "Nature gives small children an intrinsic sensibility to order, as built up by an inner sense which is a sense not of distinction between things but of distinction of the relationship between things, so that it perceives an environment as a whole with interdependent parts . . . What would be the use of an accumulation of external images without the order that brings them into organised relation? . . . It is to the child's labours that man owes the faculty, which seems a gift of nature of orienting himself, of finding his way about, in the world. In the sensitive period of order, nature gives th[is] first lesson." —*The Secret of Childhood* (page 54) by Maria Montessori

16	**Characteristics of Sensitive Periods:** "These periods correspond to special sensibilities to be found in creatures in process of development, they are transitory and confined to the acquisition of a determined characteristic. Once this characteristic has evolved, the corresponding sensibility disappears. Thus, every characteristic is established by the help of an impulse, of a transient sensibility which lasts over a limited period of growth, that is, during the corresponding sensitive period." —*The Secret of Childhood* (pages 34–5) by Maria Montessori

17	**Sensitive Period of Order at Birth:** Though what is listed here is 1–3 years old, there is considerable evidence of the newborn's sensitivity to order, especially by their eagerness for routine. The more common description of the sensitive period of order, however, is that of the toddler's deep need to *create* order. It is this manifestation of creating order that inspires the discussion in this book about the sensitive period of order between 1–3 years old. For reference, Dr. Montessori does describe the newborn's sensitivity towards order in *The Secret of Childhood* (page 59) " . . . I[t] is necessary for the adult to have studied this aspect of infant psychology, and all the more because the sensitive period of order shows itself in the first months of life."

18   **"Guides," not "Teachers":** "This is something new, especially in the educational field. It is not a question of washing the child when he is dirty, of mending or cleaning his clothes. We do not serve the child's body, because we know that if he is to develop he must do these things for himself. The basis of our teaching is that he should not be served in this sense. The child has to acquire physical independence by being self-sufficient; he must become of independent will by using in freedom his own power of choice; he must become capable of independent thought by working alone without interruption. The child's development follows a path of successive stages of independence, and our knowledge of this must guide us in our behaviour towards him. We have to help the child to act, will and think for himself. This is the art of serving the spirit . . . " —*The Absorbent Mind* (pages 292–3) by Maria Montessori

19   **Quote:** *The First 1,000 Days* (page 78) by Roger Thurow

The Plant

20   **Quote:** *The Absorbent Mind* (pages 292–3) by Maria Montessori

21   **Me:** 'Pronoun Acquisition' by Erin Vollmer MS, CCC-SLP, www.therapyworks.com

22   **I Do It!:** "When the child has been allowed a little room "in the world and in time," he proclaims as the first sign of his eager defence, 'Me! Me want to do it!' In the special environment prepared for them in our school, the children themselves found a sentence that expressed this inner need. 'Help me to do it by myself!'" —*The Secret of Childhood* (page 208) by Maria Montessori

23   **Maximum Effort!:** "Observation shows that at the age of one-and-a-half a new factor appears of great importance to the development of both arms and feet. This is the factor of strength. The child who has become active and skillful feels himself to be strong. His main idea, in whatever he does, is not merely to practise, but to exert the maximum of effort." —*The Absorbent Mind* (page 162) by Maria Montessori

The Roots: Movement

24   **Montessori & Movement:** "Let us review man's nervous system in all its amazing complexity . . . [It] has three main parts, brain, senses and muscles. Movement is the final result to which the working of all these delicate mechanisms leads up. In fact, it is only by movement that the personality can express itself." —*The Absorbent Mind* (page 144) by Maria Montessori

25   **Movement is Learning:** "Not all species on the planet have brains and if we want to know what the brain is for, we need to think about why we evolved one. Now you may reasonably think you have one to perceive or to think, but that's completely wrong. If you think about this question for any length of time, it's blindingly obvious why we have a brain: for one reason and one reason only and that's to produce adaptable and complex movements." —"The Real Reason for Brains" by Daniel Wolpert, www.ted.com

26   **Myelination:** "The axons of most neurons are coated with a fatty substance, myelin, that acts as an electrical insulator and is essential to proper information flow . . . As electrical signals race along the length of an axon, some of these ions leak out, reducing the efficiency of transmission. Myelination

solves this problem by sealing up the leaks. In fact, before they are myelinated, many fibers are incapable of transmitting impulses all the way to their endpoint, the synapse, because they lose too much ionic current along the way." —*What's Going on in There?* (page 33) by Lise Eliot

27   **Myelin Progression:** "Since the development of myelin in the spine proceeds from top to bottom, mouth, eyes, arms, and hands are used adeptly before legs and feet." —*Your Child's Growing Mind* (page 43) by Jane M. Healy

28   **Toys as Aids to Development:** "The profound difference which separates this method from the so-called "object lessons" of the old style [of teaching], is that the objects are not an aid for the mistress, who has to explain; they do not constitute means of teaching. They are an aid for the child, who chooses them himself, takes possession of them, uses them and employs himself with them according to his own tendencies and needs, just as long as he is interested in them. In this way, the objects become means of development. The objects, not the teaching given by the mistress, form the principal agent, and it is the child who uses them, who is the active being, not the teacher." —*The Discovery of the Child* (page 179) by Maria Montessori

29   **Movement Timeline:** *What's Going on in There?* (page 262) by Lise Eliot

30   **The Prepared Room:** "Order—things in their place. It means a knowledge of the arrangement of objects in the child's surroundings, a recollection of the place where each belongs. And this means that he can orient himself in his environment, possess it in all its details. We mentally possess an environment when we know it so as to find our way with our eyes shut, and find all we want within hands' reach." —*The Secret of Childhood* (page 51) by Maria Montessori

31   **Eyesight Timeline:** *What's Going on in There?* by Lise Eliot
      Range (page 210)
      Tracking (page 212)
      Color Maturation (page 216)
      Depth Perception (page 218)

32   **Movement Mat:** "If newborn infants are left on a spacious enough surface, they make very slow movements with their whole body. This active movement takes place in a clockwise direction and can be observed when there is enough space left around the infant. A single mattress of normal size will suffice, or a blanket on the ground." —*Understanding the Human Being* (page 109) by Silvana Quattrocchi Montanaro

33   **Low, Horizontal Mirror:** "The best way to help children in developing free movement in the first twelve months is to provide the large, low bed we have already described, to leave them on the ground for as long as possible, and to avoid putting them into any container that might limit their movement. There should be a mirror in the corner reserved for them, which helps children to see how they perform a movement." —*Understanding the Human Being* (pages 118–9) by Silvana Quattrocchi Montanaro

34   **Mobiles:** "The process of myelination of the nerve fibres is very quick and begins with the eye muscles. The child learns to control them in one month allowing him to follow what is happening in the environment much better. This is already an important step, since it implies a freedom to observe." —*Understanding the Human Being* (page 110) by Silvana Quattrocchi Montanaro

35   **Object Permanence & Separation Anxiety:** "Eight months is when babies are first able to retrieve a hidden toy, a feat that eludes most six-month olds. It is also when separation anxiety emerges—the way Natalie begins fussing whenever her mother leaves her sight . . . the ability known as object permanence, which is essential for attachment." —*What's Going on in There?* (page 345) by Lise Eliot

36   **The Second Basic Trust:** "Children who have freedom of movement feel they can pursue their own ideas and interests. The repeated experience of seeing an object, reaching for it and exploring it with hands and mouth, produces the reassuring sensation that when we want something we can move and go and get it." —*Understanding the Human Being* (page 126) by Silvana Quattrocchi Montanaro

37   **Self-Confidence:** "This is another important step in development which brings with it the ability to go and look for the mother whenever the child wakes up, remembers her, and wants to see her. At this point, the child no longer needs to cry in order to attract her attention. He knows what he wants (the mental idea) and is capable of obtaining it without asking but by using his ability to move and the new capacities of his body. How different is the situation of someone who is able to do what he wants by himself and that of someone who constantly has to ask for help from other people!" —*Understanding the Human Being* (pages 113–4) by Silvana Quattrocchi Montanaro

38   **The "Out of Place" Jacket Anecdote:** "The child's mother had removed her overcoat and laid it over her arm. Then the child began to shriek, and nothing could quiet him. At last I offered the mother a suggestion, namely to put her overcoat on again. This she did and the child stopped crying at once, and said happily, "Go palda," by which he meant, "Now it is all right, a coat should be worn on the shoulders." This story gives a very useful illustration of the child's wish for order and aversion to disorder." —*The Absorbent Mind* (page 134) by Maria Montessori

39   **The "Missing Plant" Anecdote:** "My mother would watch my son every Tuesday morning while I ran my community support group Baby & Me at a nearby school. Every Tuesday, my infant son and my mom would have a routine of playing downstairs and then going upstairs to do the laundry. There was a plant that lived in the middle of the stairwell as the stairs bent up to the next floor. One day, when my son was about 14 months old, they had finished playing and were headed upstairs. But my mother had taken the plant to water in the bathroom and it was, therefore, missing. My son screamed out in such a way that my mom thought he had stepped on a thumb tack. It was as sudden and piercing as if he were physically injured. She checked his whole body for injury and couldn't figure out what had happened. When she realized the plant was missing, she thought to return it and when she did, he calmed instantly and was happily ready to go upstairs." —Mariana Bissonnette

40   **The Table & Chair:** "Now-a-days, all this seems very obvious, but when I first propounded the idea people were much astonished. When I and my helpers prepared for children of three to six a world with furnishings of their own size, so that they could live in it as though it were their own home, this was thought to be absolutely wonderful. The little chairs and tables, the tiny plates and bowls for washing up, the "real life" activities of laying the table for meals . . . were hailed as wondrous innovations in the field of educational ideas." —*The Absorbent Mind* (page 175) by Maria Montessori

41   **Practical Life:** "Nothing is more astonishing than to see one of our children engaged in a so-called "exercise of practical life": completely absorbed, for example, in polishing a brass vessel and carefully following his instructions till it shines brilliantly; then without pause beginning all over again, and repeating every detail till he has polished the already shining pot several times over! This proves that the external aim was only a stimulus. The real aim was to satisfy an unconscious need, and this is why the operation is formative, for the child's repetition was laying down in his nervous system an entirely new system of controls, in other words, establishing fresh coordinations between his muscles." —*The Absorbent Mind* (page 187) by Maria Montessori

42   **Fugue & Technology:** "The mind that should have built itself up through experiences of movement, flees into fantasy. Such fugitive minds began by seeking and not finding, they wished to attach themselves to things and could not, and thus they wander among images and symbols. As for movement, these lively children are never still, but their movements are disordered, without purpose. They begin an action only to leave it unfinished, for their energy passes through things without becoming fixed on any." —*The Secret of Childhood* (page 161) by Maria Montessori

43   **Teaching Technology:** "Your overall goal should be not to "teach" your baby, but to help her discover how to organize experience for herself. The most active learners are encouraged to choose their own materials for building intelligence." —*Your Child's Growing Mind* (page 41) by Jane M. Healy

44   **Screen-time:** "Where We Stand: Screen Time" from The American Academy of Pediatrics

45   **Letting the Walking Child Walk:** "Therefore, it is clear that we must not carry the child about, but let him walk, and if his hand wishes to work we must provide him with things on which he can exercise

an intelligent activity. His own actions are what take the little one along the road to independence." —*The Absorbent Mind* (page 162) by Maria Montessori

46   **Rewards & Punishments:** "The child's training has, [teachers] think, to be guided by two reins: prizes and punishments. But if a child has to be rewarded or punished, it means he lacks the capacity to guide himself; so this has to be supplied by the teacher. But supposing he sets himself to work; then the addition of prizes and punishments is superfluous; they only offend the freedom of his spirit. Hence, in schools like ours which are dedicated to the defence of spontaneity and which aim at setting the children free, prizes and punishments obviously have no place . . . Prizes we might have abolished without serious protest. After all, this is economical; it affects few children, and then only once a year. But punishments! That is another story. These are given every day. What is meant by correcting exercise books? It means marking them from 0 to 10. How can a ["0"] correct anyone's defects? . . . To tell a child he is naughty or stupid just humiliates him; it offends and insults, but does not improve him. For if a child is to stop making mistakes, he must become more skillful, and how can he do this if, being already below standard, he is also discouraged?" —*The Absorbent Mind* (page 254) by Maria Montessori

The Roots: Language

47   **Early Communication in Language:** "There is one aspect of communication that has to be understood if adults wish to help children in a better way. All forms of communication give the child much information about the external world, about people and objects with which the child can establish a relationship, and about themselves." —*Understanding the Human Being* (page 73) by Silvana Quattrocchi Montanaro

48   **Being Heard:** "[W]e still need to develop our awareness of the meaning of communication, otherwise the sounds or signs do not really reach the person. The communication is superficial and the message is lost." —*Understanding the Human Being* (page 69) by Silvana Quattrocchi Montanaro

49   **Language Timeline:**

   Receptive Language (0–9 Months): "Centers for Disease Control's Developmental Milestones," www.cdc.gov

   Receptive Language (Knows about 50 Words): :Early Developmental Milestones: Child Development:13–18 Month Communication Milestones," www.pathways.org

   Expressive Language (0–6 Months): "Language Development: Speech Milestones for Babies," www.mayoclinic.org

   Expressive Language (6–18 Months): *What's Going on in There?* (pages 370-3) by Lise Eliot

50   **Overextension:** "Overextension in Early Language Development" by Leslie A. Rescorla, Journal of Child Language

51   **Language During Hygiene:** "Every day, there are many opportunities to say words while touching different parts of the body: at bath times and other moments of maternal care, naming objects used while preparing and serving food, or while dressing and undressing the child." —*Understanding the Human Being* (page 142) by Silvana Quattrocchi Montanaro

52   **Nouns First:** "At about a year and a half, the child discovers another fact, and that is that each thing has its own name. This shows that, from all the words he has heard, he has been able to single out the nouns, and especially the concrete nouns. What a wonderful new step to have taken! He was aware of being in a world of things, and now each of these is indicated by a special word." —*The Absorbent Mind* (page 133) by Maria Montessori

53   **Name the Experience:** "Exactly how do you know what a "dog" is? There are some pretty odd-looking dogs walking around, yet an adult can almost always say with certainty, "That's a dog." How do you know that something is a chair—and not a bench, or a stool? Somewhere inside your brain

you have mental pictures of your typical dog and chair, which you compare with each new animal or "object to sit on." If the new one is close enough to your prototype, you feel confident in using that label. Knowledge of word meanings is stored in the brain in "semantic networks" that connect millions of prototypes from things, events, and even abstract ideas such as "freedom" or "mercy." How do children develop semantic networks? From firsthand experiences with objects in the real word, and from hearing words associated with those objects." —*Your Child's Growing Mind* (page 205) by Jane M. Healy

54   **Sensitive Period of Language:** "These two studies finally give us a clear view of the critical window for language acquisition. A child's brain is maximally capable of absorbing language, particularly the rules and logic of grammar, until six or seven years of age . . . A person who is isolated from any kind of language exposure . . . will never master a single tongue." —*What's Going on in There?* (page 363) by Lise Eliot

55   **Understanding Screen-Time & Language:** "The Effects of Television on Speech Development: Does It Interfere?" by Gwen Dewar, Ph.D., www.parentingscience.com

56   **Prejudice & Discrimination in Preschool:** "Children as young as three invented complex combinations of racial meaning, for themselves and for others, and incorporated social relationships and physical characteristics to produce explanations for how their world was racially constructed and maintained. The children varied the ways in which they employed their explanations, demonstrating that they were aware of the importance of context and that they were wrestling with a multiplicity of abstractions." —*The First R: How Children Learn Race and Racism* (page 48) by Debra Van Ausdale and Joe R. Feagin

The Conditions: Eating

57   **Developmental Preparedness for Solid Food:** "For example, the stomach begins to secrete the hydrochloric acid necessary for digestion. The first tooth appears. So we see gradual perfection of the body which develops by certain processes of growth. And the result is that by six months of age the child can live without his mother's milk or at least he can combine this with other kinds of food . If we remember that before this the child was dependent entirely on maternal milk because intolerant of other food which he could not digest, we see the wonderful degree of independence that he has now reached. It is almost as though at six months he said: "I don't want to live any more on my mother. I am now fully alive and can feed myself." —*The Absorbent Mind* (page 90) by Maria Montessori

58   **The Social Side of Eating:** "If we do not use the time when feeding habits change to also change relationships, we are missing an opportunity for education and are putting obstacles in the child's road to independence . . . The parents must understand that, at about five or six months, the child has become a different human being, still small in size but much more advanced in terms of personal development." —*Understanding the Human Being* (page 93) by Silvana Quattrocchi Montanaro

59   **Teeth Eruption:** "Eruption Charts" from the American Dental Association, www.mouthhealthy.org

60   **Tongue Thrust Reflex:** "Feeding Your 4- to 7-Month-Old (for Parents)" edited by Larissa Hirsch, www.kidshealth.org

61   **Colostrum & Breast Milk:** "The medical and scientific evidence shows that breast milk provides all the energy, nutrients, and liquid that an infant needs for body and brain growth in the first six months of life. A raft of studies has found that the nutritional composition of a mother's milk adapts to her baby's needs according to the stage of development and the threats from bacteria and infections. The first milk, the colostrum, is full of vital antibodies and is essentially a child's first vaccination." —*The First 1,000 Days* (page 130) by Roger Thurow

62   **Hindmilk / Foremilk:** "Foremilk is the milk available when your baby starts feeding, hindmilk is the milk your baby gets at the end of a feed. Foremilk is not necessarily low in fat: fat content of the milk that is removed varies according to how long the milk has been collecting in the ducts and how much of your breast is drained at the time. As milk is made, fat sticks to the sides of the milk-making

cells and the watery part of the milk moves down the ducts toward your nipple, where it mixes with any milk left there from the last feed. The longer the time between feeds, the more diluted the leftover milk becomes." by La Leche League International, www.llli.org

63 **Formula & Bottle-Feeding:** "Breast-feeding advocates are absolutely right when they say that human milk was perfectly designed to nourish baby humans, and that it has unique properties that can't be replicated in formula . . . What Guilt-free Bottle-feeding aims to show you is that if you decide to feed your child formula, whether at day one or day 436, whether on its own or in combination with the breast, it is okay. You are not doing your baby any harm. You are not a bad mother . . . Our aim is simply to bring a little balance to the subject of infant feeding." —*Guilt-free Bottle Feeding: Why Your Formula-fed Baby Can Be Happy, Healthy and Smart* (page 7) by Madeleine Morris and Dr. Sasha Howard

64 **Pacing Meals:** "The child has a rhythm of his own, and this has now been recognised by child specialists, who note that children do not eat all the food they need at one go, but interpose long pauses in their slow eating. This we find already in babies before they are weaned. They stop sucking not because they have had enough, but in order to rest, for their rhythm is not only slow but intermittent." —*The Secret of Childhood* (page 187) by Maria Montessori

65 **Tastes of Fruit:** "This [squeezed, natural] fruit juice is not intended to provide vitamins or calories. It is given only as a source of additional sensory information related to food." —*Understanding the Human Being* (page 94) by Silvana Quattrocchi Montanaro

66 **Separations & Attachments:** "Birth is a great separation from all that was part of the previous environment but, if we look carefully at the situation, we can see that nature has planned birth in a way that facilitates the transition and favors its positive aspects . . . Life, in its perfection and wisdom, immediately transforms the separation of birth into a new bonding relationship which has many advantages for both the mother and her child." —*Understanding the Human Being* (pages 20-1) by Silvana Quattrocchi Montanaro

67 **Participation in the Family:** "Participation in every day life develops a feeling of worthiness in a person called upon to share it in and active way . . . The basic experience of being able to change and transform the environment gives the person a feeling of personal worth that remains forever. "I am worth something" is added to the precious feeling that "I can do things," and then becomes "I can do important things." —*Understanding the Human Being* (page 128) by Silvana Quattrocchi Montanaro

68 **Extended Breastfeeding & Nutritional Needs:** "In the transition period when breast milk or formula is no longer sufficient to meet the nutritional requirements of infants, other food and liquids are gradually introduced into the diet in what is called complimentary feeding. These 18–20 months (6–24 months in age) can mark a delicate transition; they constitute the largest portion of the 1,000 days, forming the critical period when nutrient-deficiencies and illness can cause infants to fall behind on growth charts, showing signs of stunting." —*The First 1,000 Days* (page 192) by Roger Thurow

The Conditions: Sleeping

69 **Sleep & Montessori:** In *The Secret of Childhood* (pages 69-74), Dr. Montessori has a section called "The Question of Sleep," which primarily speaks against the elongation of sleep in infants (they are made to sleep much longer than they need to) and introduces the floor bed. However, how sleep develops over time in infancy is not outlined.

70 **Sleep Needs:** "Beyond Memory: The Benefits of Sleep" by Robert Stickgold, *Scientific American*

71 **The Floor Bed:** "We therefore advise—and many families have taken our advice—that the old child's cot [a crib] should be done away with, and that in its place a very low bed should be made, which the child can enter or leave when he likes. This simple little reform will solve many difficulties that seemed hard of solution. A little, low bed, almost on the floor, is economical, like all reforms that will assist the child in his mental life, for the child needs simple things about him, and instead the few

things existing for .his sake have been complicated in a manner detrimental to him. In many families this reform has been achieved by putting a little mattress on the floor on, a big, soft carpet, with the result that children go to bed of themselves, and say good night gaily, and in the morning get up without waking anyone." —*The Secret of Childhood* (page 73) by Maria Montessori

72   **Melatonin:** "Maternal melatonin passes through the placenta, and may direct the fetus' internal clock (Torres-Farfan et al 2006). But after birth, this intimate hormonal connection is broken. Newborns must develop their own circadian rhythms of hormone production. Unfortunately for us, this takes time (Kennaway 1996), and the process is complicated by the fact that newborns need to feed every few hours. As a result, newborn sleep episodes tend to be brief, and spaced at fairly regular intervals around the clock . . . Most infants take about 12 weeks to show day-night rhythms in the production of melatonin (Rivkees 2003)." —"Newborn Sleep Patterns: A Survival Guide for the Science-Minded Parent" by Gwen Dewar, Ph.D., www.parentingscience.com

73   **Melatonin in Breast milk:** "Breastmilk contains tryptophan, an amino acid that is used by the body to manufacture melatonin. Tryptophan levels rise and fall according to maternal circadian rhythms, and when infants consume tryptophan before bedtime, they fall asleep faster (Steinberg et al 1992)." —"Newborn Sleep Patterns: A Survival Guide for the Science-Minded Parent" by Gwen Dewar, Ph.D., www.parentingscience.com

74   **Sleep Maturity at 4 Months:** "A healthy newborn (free of colic, reflux or other medical concerns) will sleep until one of three things happens: 1) hunger, 2) another need (wet/dirty diaper), 3) sleep is no longer needed . . . [S]omewhere around 3–4 months everything changes. Everything. Around this time, sleep matures. So, instead of sleep being a constant state, it becomes dynamic, and your baby will start to go through different types of sleep, called sleep stages. Sleep stages follow a predictable order that flow together in sleep cycles. These sleep cycles last about 60–90 minutes during the night (sometimes 120 minutes as they are developing) and are marked by a brief waking that happens at the end of the cycle. This brief waking is the cause of most "sleep problems." This waking is meant to be protective (adults have it too). It allows your baby to briefly check in with the environment and ask, "Am I ok?" "The 'Four-Month Sleep Regression': What Is It, and What Can Be Done About It" by Erin Flynn-Evans, Ph.D., MPH, www.babysleepscience.com

75   **Routines & Sleep:** "We propose that the implementation of a consistent bedtime routine is beneficial for many aspects of sleep in early childhood, including sleep onset latency, sleep duration, and sleep quality and consolidation, and has benefits that are just as important for overall child development and wellbeing, including health, emotional–behavioral development, literacy, parent–child interactions, and family functioning, to name just a few." —"Benefits of a Bedtime Routine in Young Children: Sleep, Development, and Beyond" by Jodi A. Mindell and Ariel A. Williamson, *Sleep Medicine Reviews*

76   **Routines & Natural Light:** "When parents include their newborns in their daily activities, newborn may adapt more rapidly to the 24-hour day (Custodio et al 2007; Lorh et al 1999) . . . Light cues might not instantly synchronize newborn sleep patterns, but they help . . . And time spent outdoors might make an important difference. Babies who go outside experience much higher daytime light levels than those kept indoors all day, and may develop stronger circadian rhythms as a result (Tsai et al 2012)." —"Newborn Sleep Patterns: A Survival Guide for the Science-Minded Parent" by Gwen Dewar, Ph.D., www.parentingscience.com

The Conditions: Hygiene

77   **Hygiene & Illness:** "One result of this poor access to safe water and improved sanitation was that one-quarter of Uganda's children suffered severe diarrhea or dysentery. Diarrhea sapped vital micronutrients out of the body and left children weaker and more vulnerable to other diseases and infections." —*The First 1,000 Days* (page 162) by Roger Thurow

78   **Bathing the Baby:** "Too many parents and adults still miss this point and handle a child solely with the aim of accomplishing, as soon as possible, the more obvious, physical tasks: changing, dressing, bathing, etc. . . . What we should do is to explain our actions to the infant, in a simple and short way,

touch the different parts of his body gently, name them and ask him to collaborate with us. This collaboration can begin from the moment of birth, but it requires a little more time and the basic trust of the child, who is an intelligent human being, eager to interact with us." —*Understanding the Human Being* (page 64) by Silvana Quattrocchi Montanaro

79   **"Least-Absorbent" Disposables:** My favorite way of explaining what type of disposable diaper would be most similar to cloth is the diaper that parents complain about and that gets "bad reviews." Mostly, the complaints are either because the diaper doesn't hold very much liquid (so there's a need for more frequent changing) or the full diaper is uncomfortable for the child. Both of these "issues" align with the intent behind using cloth diapers: the child feels discomfort with being wet and does not grow accustomed to being wet.

80   **Praise:** "Parents think they can hand children permanent confidence—like a gift—by praising their brains and talent. It doesn't work, and in fact has the opposite effect. It makes children doubt themselves as soon as anything is hard or anything goes wrong. If parents want to give their children a gift, the best things they can do is to teach their children to love challenges, be intrigued by mistakes, enjoy effort, and keep on learning. That way, their children don't have to be slaves of praise. They will have a lifelong way to build and repair their own confidence." —*Mindset: The New Psychology of Success* (pages 176-7) by Carol S. Dweck, Ph.D.

81   **Clothing for Independence:** "If we have succeeded in explaining the importance of movement, it will be obvious that appropriate clothing can do much to help a child to reach the level of motor coordination and personal independence required for the development of a happy and well-integrated human being." —*Understanding the Human Being* (page 133) by Silvana Quattrocchi Montanaro

The Gardener

82   **Bonding & Survival:** "Babies are completely at the mercy of the people who brought them into the world . . . How do babies handle these concerns? By attempting to establish a productive relationship with local power structures—you, in other words—as soon as possible. We call this attachment. During the attachment process, a baby's brain intensely monitors the caregiving it receives. It is essentially using such things as "Am I being touched? Am I fed? Who is safe?" —*Brain Rules for Baby: How to Raise a Smart and Happy Child from Zero to Five* (page 66) by Dr. John Medina

83   **The First Basic Trust:** "At the end of the symbiotic period, the child has acquired fundamental knowledge of the new environment that will always influence his vision of the world. If the vision is positive, the child will have a "basic trust" in the world and will think of it as a place where his needs can be fulfilled . . . This basic trust produces optimistic individuals who will perceive the world as a beautiful place and who believe, no matter how difficult circumstances become, that external help can be found." —*Understanding the Human Being* (page 29) by Silvana Quattrocchi Montanaro

84   **Agency:** "Believe it or not, your infant's motivational systems are already developing; one important aspect is a feeling of "agency," a term used to describe a child's sense that the world is a safe place where her efforts yield results ("When I cry for help, someone comes.") . . . Children who develop this feeling of "agency" are much more likely to develop positive motivation and become better students." —*Your Child's Growing Mind* (page 33) by Jane M. Healy

85   **Lack of Bonding:** "The inability to find safety through bonding, by a specific age in infancy, clearly caused immense stress to their systems. And that stress affected these children's behavior years later." —*Brain Rules for Baby: How to Raise a Smart and Happy Child from Zero to Five* (page 68) by Dr. John Medina

86   **Touch & Oxytocin:** "Oxytocin is for example released into the maternal circulation in response to skin-to-skin contact between mother and infant immediately after birth. The oxytocin pulses induced by skin-to-skin contact are more long lasting than those observed during labor and breastfeeding. The maternal release of oxytocin is induced by activation of sensory nerves in the skin, which are activated by

touch, warmth, and stroking in connection with skin-to-skin contact with the baby and also by massage-like hand movements performed by the baby. (Nissen et al., 1995; Matthiesen et al., 2001)." —"Self-soothing Behaviors with Particular Reference to Oxytocin Release Induced by Non-noxious Sensory Stimulation" by Kerstin Uvnäs-Moberg, Linda Handlin, and Maria Petersson, *Frontiers in Psychology*.

87   **Postpartum & Connection:** "Birth—before the advent of modern medicine—often resulted in the mother's death. Though no one knows the true figure, estimates run as high as 1 in 8. Tribes with females who could quickly relate to and trust nearby females were more likely to survive. Older females, with the wisdom of the prior birthing experiences, could care for new mothers. Women with kids could provide precious milk to a new baby if the birth mother died. Sharing and its accompanying social interactions thus provided a survival advantage, says anthropologist Sarah Hrdy . . . Females release oxytocin as part of their normal response to stress, a hormone that increases a suite of biological behaviors termed "tend and befriend" . . . Psychotherapist Ruthellen Josselson, who has studied "tend and befriend" relationships, underscores their importance: 'Every time we get overly busy with work and family, the first thing we do is let go of friendships with other women. We push them right to the back burner. That's really a mistake because women are such a source of strength to each other." —*Brain Rules for Baby: How to Raise a Smart and Happy Child from Zero to Five* (page 75) by Dr. John Medina

88   **Symbiotic Period:** "In the case of the mother and her newborn, this symbiotic life lasts 6–8 weeks and it is of great interest for us to see what these two partners can exchange. The mother provides the right food and with her presence establishes the points of reference for attachment. The newborn, on the other hand, offers the mother the reassurance that what has left her body is not lost, helps establish a referential relationship and, by suckling at the breast, helps the mother's uterus to contract and shrink back to its normal size and position." —*Understanding the Human Being* (page 28) by Silvana Quattrocchi Montanaro

89   **Four Planes:** *The Absorbent Mind* (pages 17–9) by Maria Montessori

90   **The Four Planes Charts:** At the end of her life, Montessori published two charts depicting the four planes: the Bulb and the Geometric chart that I encourage readers to look at themselves. For a non-visual explanation, the Geometric chart displays four triangles that connect each 6-year plane (0–6, 6–12, 12–18, 18–24). The triangles that connect the first (0–6) and third (12–18) are subdivided into two periods of 3 years. The endpoint of these subdivided triangles signifies the mid-point (3 and 15). In this chart, the downward line on the subdivided triangles (0–3 and 12–15) indicates development and creation. The subsequent upward line of the triangle (3–6 and 15–18) indicates a "refinement" of that development (or as Montessori called it: "the perfecting and enrichment of those powers already formed" [*The Absorbent Mind*, page 174]). The Bulb chart clearly delineates the periods of 6–12 and 18–24 as stable, developmental growth with a thin green line that runs in contrast to the fiery red bulbs of 0–6 and 12–18. These two ideas put together create this pattern: development, refinement, growth.

91   **External Pregnancy:** "The mother and child need to stay together and continue to live together because, after nine months of pregnancy, the newborn is not yet ready for an independent life. This human being is not yet capable of eating adult food or of moving at will through space . . . From the point of view of coordinated movement, the human baby is still immature and it will take 8–9 months before it will begin to crawl and be able to go any distance away from the mother . . . For this reason, the nine months after birth can be considered an "external pregnancy." —*Understanding the Human Being* (page 21) by Silvana Quattrocchi Montanaro

92   **Developmental Crisis:** In *Understanding the Human Being* (pages 148–161), Dr. Montanaro describes the "developmental crisis" in infancy: birth, weaning, and opposition. In this book, I have similarly timed "events" that I propose initiate periods of rapid development: conception, birth, mobility, and "me." Though there is some overlap in ideas, the intent of the events in the gardener's chart is to see your child in the context of the cycle of development, refinement, growth.

The Full Chart

93   Quote: *The Absorbent Mind* (page 14) by Maria Montessori

Bibliography

1. American Academy of Pediatrics. "Where We Stand: Screen Time." HealthyChildren.org, 2016. <www.healthychildren.org/English/family-life/Media/Pages/Where-We-Stand-TV-Viewing-Time.aspx>

2. American Dental Association. "Eruption Charts." Mouth Healthy TM, 2012. <www.mouthhealthy.org/en/az-topics/e/eruption-charts>

3. Blacklivesmatter.com "Herstory." Black Lives Matter, 2019. <www.blacklivesmatter.com/herstory>.

4. "CDC's Developmental Milestones." Centers for Disease Control and Prevention, 2020. <www.cdc.gov/ncbddd/actearly/milestones>

5. Dewar, Gwen. "The Effects of Television on Speech Development: Does It Interfere?" Parenting Science, 2020. <www.parentingscience.com/effects-of-television-on-children-learning-speech.html>

6. Dewar, Gwen. "Newborn Sleep Patterns." A Survival Guide, 2017. <www.parentingscience.com/newborn-sleep.html>

7. Dweck, Carol S. *Mindset*. London: Robinson, 2017.

8. Eliot, Lise. *What's Going on in There?: How the Brain and Mind Develop in the First Five Years of Life*. New York: Bantam, 2000.

9. Flynn-Evans, Erin. "The 'Four-Month Sleep Regression': What It Is and What Can Be Done About It?" Baby Sleep Science: Sleep Resource Center, 2018. < https://www.babysleepscience.com/single-post/2014/03/12/The-Four-Month-Sleep-Regression-What-is-it-and-What-can-be-Done-About-it>

10. "Foremilk and Hindmilk." La Leche League International, 2020. <www.llli.org/breastfeeding-info/foremilk-and-hindmilk>

11. Healy, Jane M. *Your Child's Growing Mind: Brain Development and Learning from Birth to Adolescence*. New York: Broadway, 2004.

12. Hirsch, Larissa. "Feeding Your 4- to 7-Month-Old (for Parents)." KidsHealth. The Nemours Foundation, 2017. <kidshealth.org/en/parents/feed47m.html>

13. Medina, John. *Brain Rules for Baby: How to Raise a Smart and Happy Child From Zero to Five*. Seattle, WA: Pear, 2014.

14. Mayo Clinic Staff. "Language Development: Speech Milestones for Babies." Mayoclinic.org, 2019. <www.mayoclinic.org/healthy-lifestyle/infant-and-toddler-health/in-depth/language-development/art-20045163>

15. Mindell, Jodi A, and Ariel A Williamson. "Benefits of a Bedtime Routine in Young Children: Sleep, Development, and beyond." Sleep Medicine Reviews. U.S. National Library of Medicine, 2018. <www.ncbi.nlm.nih.gov/pmc/articles/PMC6587181>

16. Montanaro, Silvana Quattrocchi. *Understanding the Human Being: The Importance of the First Three Years of Life*. Mountain View (CA): Nienhuis Montessori USA, 2007.

17. Montessori, Maria. *The Absorbent Mind*. Madras: Kalakshetra Publications, 1949.

18. Montessori, Maria. *The Discovery of the Child*. Adyar, India: Kalakshetra, 1949.

19. Montessori, Maria. *The Secret of Childhood*. London: Orient Longman, 1998.

20. Morris, Madeleine, and Dr. Sasha Howard. *Guilt-free Bottle-feeding: Why Your Formula-fed Baby Can Be Happy, Healthy and Smart.* Warriewood: Finch, 2014.

21. Pathways. "Early Developmental Milestones: Child Development: 13–18 Month Communication Milestones" Pathways.org, 2020. <pathways.org/growth-development/13–18-months/milestones>

22. Rescorla, Leslie A. "Overextension in Early Language Development." Journal of Child Language 7, no. 2, 1980. <repository.brynmawr.edu/cgi/viewcontent.cgi?article=1012&context=psych_pubs>

23. Stickgold, Robert. "Beyond Memory: The Benefits of Sleep." Scientific American, 2015. <www.scientificamerican.com/article/beyond-memory-the-benefits-of-sleep>.

24. Thurow, Roger. *The First 1,000 Days: A Crucial Time for Mothers and Children—And the World.* New York: PublicAffairs, 2017.

25. Uvnäs-Moberg, Kerstin, Linda Handlin, and Maria Petersson. "Self-soothing Behaviors with Particular Reference to Oxytocin Release Induced by Non-noxious Sensory Stimulation." Frontiers in Psychology. Frontiers Media S.A., 2015. <www.ncbi.nlm.nih.gov/pmc/articles/PMC4290532>

26. Van Ausdale, Debra, and Joe R. Feagin. *The First R: How Children Learn Race and Racism.* Oxford: Rowman & Littlefield, 2002.

27. Vollmer, Erin. "Pronoun Acquisition: Child Development." TherapyWorks, 2020. <www.therapyworks.com/pronoun-acquisition>

28. Wolpert, Daniel. "The Real Reason for Brains." TED Global 2011. <www.ted.com/talks/daniel_wolpert_the_real_reason_for_brains?language=en>

www.ingramcontent.com/pod-product-compliance
Lightning Source LLC
Chambersburg PA
CBHW061138230426
43662CB00022B/2459